# Praise for *Soul Searching the Millennial Generation*

"Overholt and Penner bring a unique combination of practical experience and academic expertise to this topic. Their book is consequently an informed and invaluable resource for youth workers."

> — Reginald W. Bibby, Ph.D., author of *Canada's Teens*, *Restless Gods* and *Restless Churches*

❖ ❖ ❖

"In *Soul Searching the Millennial Generation*, two proven youth advocates distill years of youth ministry wisdom into understandable principles that address the 'here and now' needs of today's young people. Each chapter is peppered with fun-to-read anecdotes, insightful trend analysis, and practical help for youth workers in the trenches.

"The authors don't pretend to have the newest gimmick for youth work, but they do present workable principles that transcend time. This book should be on the shelf of every youth worker, and should be required reading for anyone involved in lay and volunteer youth ministry roles."

> — John H. Wilkinson, Ed.D., Executive Director, Toronto Youth for Christ, and Co-ordinator, Youth Ministry Studies, Wycliffe College

❖ ❖ ❖

"Right theory without good practice distances adults from young people. Good practice without right theory is an intuitive myth. *Soul Searching the Millennial Generation* translates insightful theory into relationship-building, problem-solving practice. It is in touch with times. Read it . . . then use it!"

> — Don Posterski, co-author of *The Emerging Generation* and *Teen Trends*

❖ ❖ ❖

# Soul Searching
# the Millennial Generation

## A Guide for Youth Workers

L. David Overholt and James A. Penner

**NOVALIS**

Cover design: Caroline Gagnon
Cover image: Getty Images/Donovan Reese
Text design: Andrew Smith/Page Wave Graphics Inc.
Layout: Christiane Lemire

Published in 2005 by Novalis/Saint Paul University
Business Office:
Novalis
49 Front Street East, 2nd Floor
Toronto, Ontario, Canada
M5E 1B3

Phone: 1-800-387-7164
Fax: (514) 278-3030
E-mail: cservice@novalis-inc.com
www.novalis.ca

Published in 2002 by Stoddart Publishing Co. Limited

Library and Archives Canada Cataloguing in Publication

Overholt, L. David
    Soul searching the millennial generation : a guide for youth workers / L. David
Overholt and James A. Penner.

Includes bibliographical references and index.
ISBN 2-89507-516-6

    1. Church work with youth. I. Penner, James, 1958– II. Title.

BV4447.O94 2005          259'.23          C2004-905671-9


Printed in Canada.

We acknowledge the financial support of the Government of Canada through the Book
Publishing Industry Development Program (BPIDP) for our publishing activities.


5  4  3  2  1          09  08  07  06  05

*We would like to dedicate
this book to our families:*
Helen and Karra;
Claire, Elya, and Erick

# Contents

# Acknowledgments

We would like to thank the following people for various kinds of assistance in this writing project.

## Dave:

Helen, my wife and soul mate, and Karra, my daughter, who set aside too many afternoons of playing with her dad for "the book."

Church on the Rock, for giving freedom to their busy pastor to write and for believing in the dream of helping adolescents across our country.

Reg Bibby, who made this whole project possible.

God, who heard from me often throughout this process.

## James:

Claire, my best friend on earth, and our special children, Elya and Erick, who have stood with me throughout this venture.

The InterVarsity Christian Fellowship community, who freed me up for this project and encouraged me.

The many people who are my friends, my family, and my prayer supporters all across Canada and beyond – you know who you are.

Four mentor friends, Terese LeBlanc, Doreen Kostynuik, Reg Bibby, and Peter Hanhart, who have blessed me with their wisdom and constant support.

## Dave and James:

We are deeply grateful to Novalis for undertaking this project and appreciative of the commitment and competence of Commissioning Editor Kevin Burns in bringing the second edition of this book to fruition.

# Introduction

Because you have picked this book up, you probably love teenagers. So do we! However, loving teenagers is just the first step for those of us who work with them. We believe youth work requires two further steps.

One is understanding. We hope that as you travel through the pages of this book you will gain a deeper understanding of what forms the inner and outer worlds of the teenagers in your life, to understand their spiritual, social, and personal dispositions in the spirit of St. Francis's prayer: "Lord, help me not so much to be understood, as to understand."

The second step is creative application. We hope to spark in you the beginnings of creative thought about how you can help your teenagers. We don't want to leave you frustrated, asking, "So what do I do now?" We hope that our creative applications of theory into actual youth work will help you create your own applications to your own situations.

We are both lifelong seasoned youth workers. Dave is a pastor of a youth-targeted church of many hundreds. He heads up the youth and family department at Tynedale Seminary and speaks extensively to youth and youth workers in Canada and the United States. James is a para-church youth worker who teaches a sociology of youth course at University of Lethbridge, Alberta, and is a spiritual director and youth culture/ministry consultant in Canada. Dave has a doctorate in Philosophy of Education with a dissertation on the dynamics of adult-teen mentoring. James has a master's degree in sociology, with a thesis on the relationship (or lack thereof) between teens and organized religion. We both have extensive training at various colleges, seminaries, and retreat centres. And we were both invited by renowned sociologist Reginald W. Bibby to take his recent nation-wide teen survey and apply it to youth work.

We bring different strengths to this venture. Because of his sociological background, James contributed much of the survey analysis, while Dave, because of his more extensive and intensive front-line experience in youth ministry, contributed the bulk (but not all) of the youth ministry stories and insights. The "I" in this book is used interchangeably, but it most often refers to Dave's experiences. We have analyzed teen culture through different lenses – James through a sociological lens and Dave through a psychological/educational lens. To us, this book is very much "co-authored art," with all of the advantages, joint commitment, ongoing communication, and tradeoffs that such a venture implies.

Both of us assume that God is still very much alive and lovingly working in individuals and communities. Both of us have joyfully experienced the God who tasted death and lives again: Jesus Christ. We are writing this book with an understanding that there is a partnership with God in youth ministry. You may not share this assumption. We respect that. Still, we invite you, "Please read on!" The Christian community has a very active history in working with teenagers, and we believe that you may gain insight into your group by observing ours. We have tested our findings with a large sampling of Catholics, Mainline Protestants, and Evangelicals, and found that our analyses and their implications to ministry can be broadly applied.[1] But they can be applied outside church circles as well, places such as the family, community youth programs, schools, sports settings, and the work arena.

## Sources

The sources of our research are threefold.

First, we have used Reginald Bibby's Project Teen Canada (PTC) 2000, 1992, 1984, survey data. This unparalleled source of comprehensive trend data, published in his book *Canada's Teens* (2001), shines a light on the values, behaviours, expectations, and concerns of young people over the past two decades. In addition, we occasionally used Reg's Project Canada (PC) 2000 adult survey to compare today's teens with today's young adults, parents, and grandparents.

Surveys can be likened to aerial photos, freezing images in time from an airplane at 30,000 feet. No research tool is better for establishing cultural and generational patterns on a macro level and understanding the shifting trends of an entire society. However, surveys are what researchers call "thin" description (as opposed to the "thick" description of face-to-face interaction). The surveys we used for this book do not fully describe our teens. Few people wish to be defined merely as a member of a cohort. Youth and young adults are complex, unique, and awe-inspiring individuals. The greatest survey data in the world can provide only limited information on specific youth. It cannot begin to match what can be accomplished by sipping a Coke or cappuccino across the table from a youth. But the surveys do give us a great starting point for the job of getting to know teenagers one person at a time.

As we immersed ourselves in the data and reflected on our youth ministry experiences, nine key themes emerged:

- the supremacy of relationships;
- the effectiveness of authority figures;
- a desire to break free from childhood restrictions;
- the omnipresence of popular culture, as defined by music, movies, and television;
- the pressure to consume;
- experience with new technologies;
- teen concerns;
- a romantic notion of risk;
- subtle shifts in values and language.

Each of these topics forms a chapter of the book. The last chapter is a summary of youth ministry principles that worked as background assumptions.

We are extremely pleased to be able to offer Canadian data and ideas to Canadian youth workers. However, we are convinced this resource speaks to youth workers in the United States. Canada is farther down the multicultural, relativistic road some call postmodernism,[2] and perhaps has something strategic to share about youth ministry from experience in an increasingly diverse and global context. As an American friend across the border told me, "We in the States are seeing this postmodern wave coming; you in Canada have been living in it."

Our second source of information is face-to-face interactions with countless young people and youth leaders. We have spent our entire adult lives mentoring and educating youth and young adults in faith communities and professional settings. We have lived the question "How can adults and youth together experience life that is fully human and joyfully alive?" The practical applications sprinkled through these pages come from years spent pursuing this question. We have confidence that what we have learned can be applied across the board.

Last, but not least, we have consulted the Bible. As Donald Posterski has said, "The Bible as God's permanent revelation establishes the agenda for ministry. Faithful people will always aim to implement what it teaches."[3] We have tried to think biblically about each topic addressed. In particular, we studied the New Testament eyewitness accounts of Jesus, and sought out theologians and practitioners who could help us address this question: "Given the trends in youth culture today, how would Jesus encourage his followers to respond to today's young people?"

## Structure

Each chapter of the book begins with a cluster of findings from the PTC survey. We then look at the large-scale pattern that emerges and ask, "Why are teens doing the things they do?" But because we strive to go beyond simply understanding teenagers, the bulk of each chapter suggests creative strategies for adults who work with youth, asking, "How can we propel this generation toward liberating, joy-filled adulthood and spiritual maturity?" At the end of each chapter we include a to-do list that will help you achieve these goals.

## Youth Work as Mission Work

Teen culture is different from mainstream culture. It frequently shocks adults. Our first response to teen culture is often that there is something wrong with it, that it needs to be transformed into something that looks more like our adult culture. Yet we would never think of suggesting there is something wrong with Europeans or Asians just because they eat, dress, or speak differently from us. We must remember that, in many respects, youth work is cross-cultural.

The challenge we face as adult youth workers is to honour teen culture as a creative expression of who teens are, while realizing that elements of that culture may be unhealthy. Some who read this book will think we are simply accepting teen culture and allowing it to set the agenda of ministry to teens. To such readers we say, yes, we are – as we would hope to do if we were working in a foreign culture. We would allow that culture to set the language and dress, and select the agenda of the message (which contains a multitude of messages). Other readers will question passages in which we seek to transform and bring a message to teen culture. To these people we say, yes – there are elements of any society that are not healthy, and our message does have a transformative and prophetic role to play. Of course, we won't always get it right. Still, we focus on making what we think are the most helpful recommendations.

Finally, we want to welcome you to this adventure of soul searching the millennial generation. If you're reading this, chances are you're already a front-line youth worker or a parent of one or more youth. Bottom line: You care a lot about the younger generation. Many of you care enough to be frantic, exhausted and poor in order to launch those you love in the millennial fold. We know you are there – hundreds upon hundreds of selfless parents, volunteers, and professionals. We've met you – community and campus youth workers, youth group sponsors, counsellors, camp cabin leaders, moms and dads, Sunday school teachers, educators, municipal government leaders, clergy, informal friends of youth, and college students strategically training to be youth pastors and/or youth professionals. All of you are doing your best to create meaningful communities and assist significant faith and life commitments among youth and young adults. As you touch young people one at a time in mentoring relationships and corporately in youth groups, you are steering the course of the twenty-first century in eternally good ways. Our world will be better ten years from now because of your efforts. *Bravo!* We hope you thoroughly enjoy reading and applying this book.

*Dave and James*

# CHAPTER ONE

# The Millennials

Ll across North America, thousands of youth groups will meet tonight. Youth leaders will make frantic last-minute phone calls after learning that the pizza place won't deliver, or that seventeen teens have shown up, when the van they reserved holds only fifteen people. Later on, hundreds of junior and senior high-school students will be talking about their teenage realities over a Coke with adults they trust. Somewhere tonight a youth will decide not to kill him- or herself because of the presence of a caring adult. For still others, new possibilities will take root tonight when a simple word of encouragement fertilizes the seeds of a dream.

## Who Are the Millennials?

Today, 4.1 million Canadian and 40 million American youth and young adults crave that "I believe in you" message from adults and peers. They are part of what social analysts refer to as the "millennials." Born in the 1980s and 90s, this generation is coming of age as we begin our journey through the third millennium.[1]

They are a large cohort – a second baby boom of sorts. Neil Howe and William Strauss comment, "As a group, Millennials are unlike any other youth generation in living memory. They are more numerous, more affluent, better educated, and more ethnically diverse."[2] Because of the sheer size of this group and the desire of virtually every social institution to pass on its values, attitudes, and products, adults have a deep desire to understand and influence the millennials.

This inspirational generation has much to teach us. These teenagers have high self-esteem and great expectations for their personal future. Some recent commentators go so far as to say that this generation will alter our social landscape in significantly positive ways. As Howe and Strauss put it, "Over the next decade, the Millennial Generation will entirely recast the image of youth from downbeat and alienated to upbeat and engaged – with potentially seismic consequences for America."[3]

While only a third of millennials claim to have experienced God (36%), many more believe that spirituality is important (60%). This belief creates a hunger to experience God. To our great wonder, millennials are open to experiences through religious institutions. When teens who did not attend services at least once a month were given the statement, "I'd be open to more involvement with religious groups if I found it to be worthwhile," nearly 40% said they would be interested. If the Quebec data are excluded from the total, the figure jumps closer to 50%. What a great open door to find out how we can mutually meet each other's needs! If corporations were to learn that 40% of consumers were interested in them, they would pour all their resources into reaching that market share. There is a strategic opportunity for youth ministry by faith groups.

Thirteen percent of teens take part in religious youth groups; 87% do not. Of the teens who are in religious youth groups,

- 63% are Protestant
- 20% are Catholic
- 14% belong to other faiths
- 3% claim no religious affiliation, although they participate in the youth group of a particular religion.

Teens who participate in religious youth groups and emerging churches are much more likely to enjoy their religion, value religious group involvement, believe in God, believe that God cares about them, experience God's presence, and display high levels of honesty, politeness, and compassion than either regular church attenders who do not belong to religious youth groups or non-church attenders. These findings suggest that youth groups in which teens and adults experience life and explore faith together go a long way toward enhancing the lives of today's teens.[4]

## Developmental Issues

Some things the survey points to are not so much generational as developmental. In other words, some of the findings are there simply because today's millennials are teenagers. We will try to distinguish between those issues that are simply part of being a teenager and those that have been produced by a special cultural condition.

According to psycho-social theorist Erik Erikson, the teen years are when people deal with identity issues, when they figure out who they believe they are. Once teens have begun to resolve identity, intimacy issues become paramount during the young adult years. They determine who their real friends are and who is committed to staying connected with them through thick and thin. Ideally, youth have the opportunity at this time to discover a caring lifelong community. This affiliation not only affords them the opportunity to establish a nurturing relationship with God, but also teaches them that walking through life with like-minded sojourners can add meaning and purpose to existence.

An adolescent is in the throes of a physical, psychological, and sociological change. As Rolf E. Muuss, Eli Velder, and Harriet Porten have written,

> Sociologically, adolescence is the transition period from dependent childhood to self-sufficient adulthood. Psychologically, it is a "marginal situation" in which new adjustments have to be made, namely those that distinguish child behavior from adult behavior in a given society. Chronologically, it is the time span from approximately twelve or thirteen to the early twenties, with wide individual and cultural variation.[5]

It bears repeating: The years of adolescence are transition years. By the end of them, a youth has made the monumental move from the security (or insecurity!) of the home to full-fledged maturity, when resourcefulness and responsibility kick in. At the same time, the youth has moved from having the body and mind of a child to having those of an adult. This transition is a daunting one!

Because adolescence is also a sociological creation, its boundaries change. The survey focused on youths between the ages of fifteen and nineteen. Many people, however, believe that adolescence of a sort extends past high school, especially when a teen goes directly to college or university. They don't consider the cultural transition from childhood to adulthood complete until the youth has some kind of job, is married and/or living on his or her own, and is contributing to the wider society. Students in colleges and universities are frequently seen, even by themselves, as in some way putting off entering "real life." They are in an extended adolescence – what James Côté and Anton Allahar call a "generation on hold."[6]

## The Stress of Transition

"Next year I want to be thir-'kid', not thir-'teen,'" said one twelve-year-old.

Have you ever taken a stress test, where you assign yourself $x$ number of points of stress if you have moved, had a death in the family, or changed jobs? In these tests, stress is linked to significant life changes. In adolescence, we inevitably experience significant changes, sometimes on a daily basis. Teen bodies are perceptibly changing. Breasts start growing (and showing). Pubic hair can't be hidden in locker rooms. Periods and wet dreams confuse. Girls start to experience the gaze of grown men. Magazines and corporations start to market to this age group with a vengeance, using exaggerated notions of "femininity" and "masculinity" right when youth are most vulnerable. Teens are changing in the way they think, focusing on the ideal possibilities of life. Because of hormonal changes, teens start to see each other as sexual beings. First loves, first jobs all happen during this time. Teens have aspirations they have never had before. School turns up the pressure to perform several notches. Team sports, drama ensembles, musical groups, and friendship groups all add pressure along with their promises of successful, happy futures. If you gave each change a stress number, many teens would be off the chart. In fact, stress level related to "so many things changing" is higher for youth than any generation of adults today.

TABLE 1.1 **Personal Concern Across Generations**

(% indicating bothered "A Great Deal" or "Quite a Bit" about so many things changing)

| Teens | 38 | Parents | 24 |
|---|---|---|---|
| Young adults | 19 | Grandparents | 25 |

*Bibby,* Canada's Teens, *2001: 240*

We adults often repress our memories of the lack of confidence, the constant comparing, the teasing, the bullying of junior/senior high years. Take a minute now to remember your own adolescence. You will probably recall the inner confusion in that personal struggle to attain a worthwhile and sturdy identity you could proudly call your own.

I have just finished marking a whole stack of papers from a class of adults who were asked to remember their own adolescence. Every one of them wrote that they'd in some way struggled with periods of low self-esteem and self-doubt. One wrote that high school changed her life forever, as she "linked her dreams to her inability." Each student believed he or she alone had experienced the waters of self-doubt and was astounded to learn that every other person in the class had shared this experience.

A speech from the award-winning Lethbridge Collegiate Institute drama *Kids Will Be Kids* says,

> School sometimes makes you feel like a statistic. We travel in mass hysteria, hoping that nothing outside the usual rigor will occur. Being harassed about a fashion flop, an embarrassing occurrence…or perhaps…a random act of violence provoked by nothing. Insults are thrown, the threat intended for egos to be built or to be bruised. Stars are born by a glorified name gained from an exaggerated rumor. To be allowed into a clique, one must prove worthiness by the set standard. If you're not one or the other what are you? Non-existent. An unknown face invisible to the people around you. From my recollection of junior high the part that sticks in my mind is the constant immaturity. By high school some people just get taller.[7]

Youth, by definition, is the transition from dependent childhood to responsible adulthood. In this strategic time, where ambiguity is a given and stress levels are high, responsible adults have a pivotal, life-expanding role to play.

## The Importance of Youth Ministry

I lead wilderness orienteering. For those who are uninitiated, orienteering involves arriving at a certain point in the forest (a food drop-off zone) by following the heading of a compass. If you are off by one degree when you start your journey, you could be thousands of feet off after walking five miles. Similarly, changes that at first seem small can in fact point a teen's whole life in a different direction. That "simple" change in direction can affect hundreds of people he or she comes into contact with over the course of a lifetime. My friend and co-worker Steve Brown says that when he is at a campfire with teens he squints, and sees through the smoke that each student is a representative of hundreds of people who stand behind him or her, waiting to be influenced. This is the art, and the wonder, of youth ministry.

Try this little experiment. Think about someone who influenced you toward your job, your hobbies. Chances are that influence stretches back into your teen years. For example, I recently enjoyed speaking at a camp in Albany, New York. I had the opportunity to speak there because of a friendship I made during my first job in western New York State. I had that job because of the college I attended. I attended that college because a friend at camp told me about it. I went to that camp because of a split-second decision my dad asked me to make when I was sixteen.

What happened in your teen years? What marble did you step on that swung you around and changed everything? Youth workers, along with their students, are creating turning points that change lives and change nations.

Last fall I had lunch with Rev. Dale Lang, who has been propelled to national prominence in Canada since his son was tragically gunned down in a high school. Dale has travelled across Canada and has addressed more than 100,000 students with a message of hope and forgiveness. Dale shared with me his vision of a coming "nameless" revival of ordinary people, each catching the importance of putting other people ahead of things and issues. "Everything positive happens one heart at a time," Dale stated simply. "No ministry we do is less significant than any other!"

Can you imagine the slow, exponential building of a tidal wave of compassion, as people are starting to be faithfully available to the young (and older!) people in their orbit? By touching one heart at a time, you and I can become just such nameless heroes.

All youth work is really mission work. In my church, which services many other churches, we lose a quarter of our attenders every year. Many of the teenagers head off to college. Our university students head back home, or to different cities to find work. The teens in your church right now will not likely be the volunteer deacons and elders in that church years from now. However, they *will* be the volunteer deacons and elders in somebody's church. We have to stop seeing teen work as ownership, and start seeing the reality: that teen work is mission work for a nation.

When that great young couple comes into your church, or the highly trained single person sits in a pew for the first time, how many of you ask, "What made them the way they are?" The answer is that some adult or youth group somewhere did their job. Perhaps falling attendance figures in churches are the result of many years where youth ministry was not taken seriously.

If you work with youth in a faith community, you are uniquely situated to be a meaningful and transformational presence in the life of someone young. And you are making a difference! Many youth we've encountered in our travels across North America are profoundly joyful that you are there. I especially remember two youth groups I visited one spring. Joy and healthy relationships permeated these communities. They were "colonies, islands of one culture in the middle of another," outposts of an arena where freedom and compassion reigned. Youth in these communities stated over and over that their group was a safe and fun place where they could make and bring friends, be themselves, explore God, and make a difference in their world. Each group had strategic, sacrificial, and caring adults present. I hope that many more such intergenerational communities will be created as time goes on.

## Sobering Realities for Churches

Youth work is a God-sized challenge. The national survey data suggest that only 20% of teens feel joyful when they think of faith communities.

**Teen Enjoyment from Religious Groups**

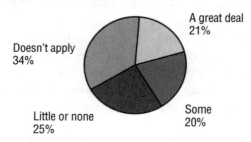

A great deal
21%

Doesn't apply
34%

Little or none
25%

Some
20%

The national picture suggests that approximately one-third of the teen population has no connection to a religious group, and another quarter is unimpressed with the impact religion is having on their lives.

This sobering reality was driven home for me in an unchurched teen focus group I conducted. One teen stated, "Tell church leaders to leave us alone. If they pester us too much, we'll tell them to 'F off.' If we have questions, we'll come to you." But when I asked that same group the question, "What comes to your mind when you think of religious leaders, ministers, priests, and pastors?" the room went quiet for a few seconds. They were thinking hard. Then I got three responses: "The Pope, that's the only one I can think of!" "The guy on TV who bumps you on the forehead and you fall over – we don't need that kind of religion!" and "The ones who come to your doors in twos. They're pushy." At that moment I realized something very significant: Many teens have absolutely no clue what happens within those religious groups where teens do report contentment.

With God helping us, we must do a way better job of uncovering what happens in joy-producing religious youth groups, spread the news around, and find ways to make these places more available to all types of youth. At the same time, some things that have been done supposedly "in the name of Jesus" have to stop.

At one churched focus group, I mentioned the "leave us alone" comment. An articulate young woman reinforced for me how pestering some religious youth groups really are. In the group she previously attended, "If you didn't believe the same things they believed, they stated that you were going to hell. I will never go back to a group like that." Another bright God-seeking youth we consulted for this book said a youth worker at his previous church had judged him as a "bad kid." He then drifted to another group, but didn't click with the youth worker who, he sensed, felt hurt when he left. He now attends another church with his parents, but finds little or no value in his present experience because "the youth group was cliquey." He then added, "Two coffees with you have done more for me than three years of youth groups."

I wish I could say that all the teens who have contacted me over the years were this affirming. I've learned the hard way what does and does not work with youth. Taking the time for informal relationships is key. Long-term, non-judgmental relationships of unshockable friendship with youth are a *must*.

There's a big job ahead of us – a challenge that needs us all – and the picture will change only slowly, one positive contact at a time. So strap on your seat belts as we attempt to describe this generation of teenagers and its needs and possibilities in more depth.

CHAPTER TWO

# Friendship Tribes and Lego Connections

I t is one o'clock in the morning and I am sitting in the gutter with an eighteen-year-old man. He is not really crying – howling would be a better word. His girlfriend has just broken up with him. We are sitting on the curb across the street from her house. Slash marks are still fresh on his wrists. In between his howls of emotional pain, we observe her friends going in and out to comfort her. At times there is a traffic jam on her front lawn. Where do they all come from at one in the morning?

The young man and I go for a walk, away from the scene of the crime, as it were. After his howls turn to cries, he assures me that his life is over. He has lost not only his girlfriend, but also the group of friends they shared. The front-lawn traffic made it obvious that she was in the friendship clan and he was out. I was walking beside a tribesperson sent away from the clan. Every adult voice in me wanted to cry out, "It's only a group of friends. You'll find other ones!" But I knew too much to say such a thing; I knew that teens value friendship more than almost anything else.

## Survey Says: Nothing Rates Higher Than Friendship

TABLE 2.1 **Teen Values**

- 85% of teens state that friendship is "very important" to them. No other value is higher.

- 94% of teens get "a great deal" or "quite a bit" of enjoyment from their friends. No other enjoyment is higher.

- 93% of teens are spending time with friends every week, and 60% are with friends daily. Few other activities happen as or more often.

- 55% of teens choose friends as the first place to turn when facing a serious problem. 43% choose family. Nothing else even comes close.

| TOP TEN TEEN VALUES | TOP TEN WEEKLY ACTIVITIES |
|---|---|
| #1. Friendship | #1. Watch television |
| #2. Freedom | #2. Listen to music |
| #3. Being loved | #3. Spend time with friends |
| #4. Having choices | #4. Do homework |
| #5. Honesty | #5. Stay in shape |
| #6. Humour | #6. Use a computer |
| #7. Comfortable life | #6. Sit and think |
| #8. Success | #8. Keep up with news |
| #9. Cleanliness | #9. Access web sites |
| #10. Concern for others | #10. Watch videos at home |

| TOP TEN TEEN ENJOYMENTS | TOP FIVE TEEN SOURCES OF SUPPORT |
|---|---|
| #1. Friends | #1. Friends |
| #2. Music | #2. Family |
| #3. Your own room | #3. Self |
| #4. Your mother | #4. God |
| #5. Dating | #5. No one |
| #6. Sports | |
| #7. Your father | |
| #8. Boy/girlfriend | |
| #9. Television | |
| #10. Brothers/Sisters | *Bibby,* Canada's Teens, *2001: 13ff* |

Simply put, teens place greater importance on friendship than on any other value. Teens enjoy nothing more than leisure time with friends, and few things are given as much time. In addition, most teens turn to friends when in trouble. First in values, first in enjoyment, first as a source of support – let this sink in for a moment: Friendships are absolutely monumental for teens! Think for a moment about what you value most, whether it is faith, your life's work, or family. Now imagine losing it. That's how strongly teenagers feel about their friends. As Donald Posterski writes, "Friendship is the glue that holds youth culture together."[1]

## Friendship Tribes and Lego Connections

Teenagers need to feel a "snap" of connections with others, like the snap of Lego blocks fitting together in the hands of a child. Lone teens feel but one pressing need: to be connected. Yet, like Lego, teens have only so many points of connection built into them, with the number of points dependent on individual personality. Some teens have only one very close friend; more often, teens cluster in larger "tribes." Nine in ten teens have at least two close friends, while half acknowledge four or more.

Tribe members may choose nicknames (or be given nicknames by their peers) that relate to their cultural role, whether they be skaters, geeks, Goths, or drama-mamas. A tribe has its own rituals of membership, stories that glue members together (myths), symbols of dress that reflect group values. A college student I talked to remembered discovering "mod" music many years ago. He loved it, and the enjoyment of this music gave him entrance into a tribe, where he was instantly and powerfully drawn into a whole way of dressing, acting, and understanding life. Joining this tribe meant buying into its distinct philosophy.

TABLE 2.2 **The Influence of Friends**

| |
| --- |
| • 91% of teens have two or more close friends.<br>52% have four or more close friends.<br>3% have none. |
| • 39% of males and 53% of females are bothered "quite a bit" or "a great deal" at the thought of losing friends. |
| • 78% of teens state that friends have "quite a bit" or "a great deal" of influence on them. Only upbringing (91%), willpower (89%), and mother (81%) are rated higher. |

*Bibby, PTC 2000 data set*

Tribes often contain many "clans" of four to five close friends. These are the carloads of peers that go shopping or to the movies, or that hang out talking at the local variety store. Increasingly, these clans include teens of both sexes. They are usually based on similar histories or common interests. A clan may form in Grade 9 as a group of friends that graduated from the same elementary school, but will change shape over the years as the members' common interests fluctuate. I have found that late Grade 9 for girls and early Grade 10 for boys are common times when students will peel away from one clan and go looking for another to join. These moments when teens switch peer groups may be the most significant moments in a teen's life, charged with possibility for positive change. (Some teens have membership in several clans at the same time. We call these young people "connectors," and will look at their significance later in this chapter.)

Walking through Forest, a small town in Ontario, I passed the local high school just as it let out for lunch. The students streamed, in their friendship clans, along various side streets. As they converged onto a main street, the clans nearly bumped into each other, yet no one acknowledged anyone in another clan. Based on their treatment of each other, these teens could have been complete strangers, although many of them, in all likelihood, shared the same classes. In a relational subculture, the specific clan and more general tribe provide the most important focus for teens. Others in their world go unnoticed.

Friendship clusters seem to have a shorter life span than they once did. Current television shows portray an idealistic level of intimacy among friends that leaves teens disillusioned with their own clans. In real life, friends tend to come and go.

## Relationship Stability and Stress

Friendship may take the top position, but it does come with its share of stress. Teens intuitively know the importance of relationships, but they haven't necessarily learned to cherish the values needed to maintain these relationships. As seen in Table 2.3, many of the teens in the survey valued receiving love (friendship, being loved, etc.) more highly than giving it (generosity, concern for others, etc.).

TABLE 2.3 **Friendship by Gender**

| Values (% rating as "Very Important") | Male | Female |
|---|---|---|
| Friendship | 80 | 90 |
| Being loved | 65 | 87 |
| Concern for others | 51 | 73 |
| Generosity | 37 | 47 |
| Concerns (% rating "Quite a Bit" or more) | Male | Female |
| Losing friends | 39 | 53 |
| Not having a boy/girlfriend | 36 | 32 |

Bibby, Canada's Teens, 2001: 13, 16, 19

Instability in their friendships is a monumental concern to teenagers. As we look at the faces of our young people, we can know that 50% of females and 40% of males will be concerned over losing a friend.[2] (Some are concerned over the recent loss of a specific friend, while others are more generally afraid of losing friends in the future.) Ostracism from one's tribe or clan is a primal stress.

Some teenagers find building relationships so stressful that they become paralyzed in the process. Amy was such a girl. One summer evening, she told me she had gone through high school alone. She was a great young woman, and I wondered why she considered herself friendless. She told me that she had waited for – hoped for – that one special "best friend." Waiting and worrying, she never developed any of her acquaintances, and so went through four years feeling alone.

A third of teens are also deeply concerned about their ability to secure a soulmate of the opposite sex. Finding romantic love is a key intimacy issue during the teens and twenties, and many youth fear they will fail at this endeavour.

## The Impact of Family vs. Peer Friendship

Although peers do have a significant influence on the lives of teens, Table 2.4 demonstrates that teens perceive their upbringing, their own willpower, and their mothers as being more influential than friends. And their fathers are not far behind. This is a significant finding: Peer influence is not as overpowering as we have at times concluded.

TABLE 2.4 **Top Ten Teen Perceived Sources of Influence**

(% perceive it as influencing their lives "A Great Deal" or "Quite a Bit")

| | |
|---|---|
| #1. | The way you were brought up — 91 |
| #2. | Your own willpower — 89 |
| #3. | Your mother specifically — 81 |
| #4. | Your friend(s) — 78 |
| #5. | The characteristics you were born with — 71 |
| #6. | Your father specifically — 70 |
| #7. | Another adult you respect — 58 |
| #8. | Music — 53 |
| #9. | What you read — 43 |
| #10. | God or some other supernatural force — 40 |

*Bibby,* Canada's Teens, *2001: 31*

In my seminary class I give an exercise in which the students write down their top five values. They then place checkmarks beside the values that are also important to their parents. On average, my students share four out of five values with their parents.

Many teens have made hard decisions to leave peer groups they deem to be a negative influence. In our experience, the strength of the family (or a new peer group) is a key factor in a teen's decision to leave an unhealthy tribe and clan. The tribes and clans of teens may shift throughout their junior/senior high-school experience, but the security of strong family relationships lends stability amidst otherwise volatile circumstances.

Parents should ask themselves what values they are displaying to their kids. If you ask your children what they think you value most, you may be surprised at their answers. Our values more often show through our actions than through our words.

## Adult-Teen Friendships

Growing up involves evaluation and reshaping childhood values. Teens generally do this outside the family in the peer arena; however, if caring adults are present and interactive, many teens will gladly turn to them. A key topic in this book is the role that adult-teen mentoring relationships can play in youth work. While the survey did not address this directly, we believe strong adult-teen relationships play a significant role in the lives of many teens. In a society that appears to have a genuine generation gap, most teens report that adults lack respect for them. Many of these same teens, however, point to an individual adult beyond their immediate family who is having a significant impact on them.

### TABLE 2.5 **Adult Influence**

| |
| --- |
| • Only 33% of males and 25% of females believe that adults respect their opinions. |
| • 58% of both males and females state that an adult they respect has influenced them "a great deal" or "quite a bit." |

*Bibby, PTC 2000 data set*

## Why Is This the Case?

Friendships, and especially peer friendships, are important to teens for key theological, psychological, and sociological reasons.

Theologically, healthy relationships are at the core of the universe. According to the biblical record, creator God (father, son, and spirit) is the original friendship cluster. The primary personality of the universe, God, is what the Hebrews called *Hased* (affectionate and loyal) and the New Testament writers called *Agape* (generous and kind). Since adolescents (and all other humans) are made in the image of this relational deity, they fundamentally find meaning in intimate relationships – thus the need for connection points. It should not surprise us that friendship scores at the top of the chart for teens today. Friends always have been, and always will be, of prime importance. We adults, so interested in the business of "getting ahead," might be missing the point of remaining connected beings.

Psychologically, adolescents are in a transition period. They are moving from being children (but call them children, and they may never forgive you) to the world of adults, and beginning the process of discovering who they want to be. They still believe, though often naively, that anything is open to them, that they can be anyone they want to be. As adolescence unfolds, young people increasingly look beyond the home for answers to their most fundamental questions: "Who am I?" "Who are my people?" "Which tribe will I be a part of, so that through membership I can express my identity?" Note, however, that for the most part adolescents are not rejecting their families; they are simply starting to value outside socialization forces in their discovery attempts. (This phenomenon is explored more deeply in Chapter Four.)

Sociologically, teens are segregated from the rest of society. This can be observed in the marketing, educational, and family realities of today's youth. "Until the rise of American advertising, it never occurred to anyone anywhere in the world that the teenager was a captive in a hostile world of adults," says Gore Vidal.[3] Our capitalist system itself benefits from and subtly encourages teen segregation. If you create a sub-group (such as youth), you can then market to it. Hence, massive energies are poured into defining a youth culture that is distinct from others, so as to successfully create and promote youthful products.

Whatever its origins, adolescence is experienced in what journalist Patricia Hersch has aptly called "a tribe apart."[4] It is easier today for teens to have relationships with each other than with adults. Most teens experience schooling in classrooms segregated by age. Parents and other adults are kept away from children and teens by their jobs and other responsibilities. Whether by default or by design, intergenerational connections are devalued.

## What Does This Mean for Youth Work?

One veteran youth pastor started every youth-volunteer meeting with the question "What are the five principles of youth work?" The adult volunteers would all repeat the mantra "Relationships, relationships, relationships, relationships, relationships!" This youth worker was not far off the mark. Our task, as youth workers, is to help teens make and maintain those Lego connections mentioned earlier, both with each other and with the adults in their lives.

## Connect Teens with Adults

Many first-time adult volunteers come out to a youth night wanting to help – but they expect to be asked to perform tasks. When I ask them to sit down and get to know a teenager, they look at me as if I have just asked them to swim across an ocean! Some will say, "Okay, I can do that, but what can I really do to help?" My answer is the same, "Sit down, run around, get a pie in the face if you have to, but build relationships."

Leisurely "ministry of presence" by a vulnerable you is more valuable than the execution of tasks. The better your relationships with adolescents, the greater the chance they will model themselves after you, learn from lessons you give them, come to you for help, take your advice, be unafraid to be vulnerable in front of you, and so on. "Teenagers are crying out – or wanting to cry out but are afraid that no one is listening – as never before for meaningful relationships. They crave genuine connections based on real love,"[5] writes Dawson McAllister.

While relationships between teens and twenty-somethings can form with relative ease, intergenerational connections need not be limited to these age groups. Many of our best youth volunteers are in their thirties and forties. Recently, our community teenagers asked to have older adults return to our "student-led" ministry. They had fun with the twenty-somethings, but long for the aged-based wisdom during times of crisis. Seniors also have much to teach youth about life and God. They've walked many miles through lots of hardships – and at times they are right under your nose. When I was a teen, one of the best youth workers in my church was an eighty-something named Gramma Hammond. She would hobble out the back doors of the church and ask for my arm. She then had me for a good ten minutes, as we walked at a leisurely pace toward her car. She would look up at me and tell me whom she had shared her faith in Jesus with that week. She wistfully looked forward to the day she was bed-ridden, when the people surrounding her would be able to listen undistracted to her stories of faith. Her strong relationship with Jesus, and the strong relationship she built with me during our walks, marked my soul by modelling an active faith to me.

Relationship-building is the heart of youth ministry – everything else is trappings!

## Build a Team Around You

As any given Lego piece has limited number of connection points, so every person has a limited capacity for close friendships. Particularly strong friendships use up more of this capacity, clicking into place at more than one connection point, as it were. But once an individual's capacity for intimate relationships has been reached, new friendships cannot form until ties with old friends are broken.

We leaders also have a limited number of connecting points – we cannot get to know everyone in our youth groups. We need others to work with us. I used to enjoy doing youth ministry by myself. It was easier than explaining it to others. Although people around me sometimes wondered why I was on my own, I fooled myself into thinking no one really wanted to help out. Finally, when a college student begged me to let him help, I allowed him to do some goofy announcements. Attendance increased. Some of the new students identified more with him, or they found that he had more time for them. I had been holding back the growth of the group by the number and type of connecting points I had.

New youth workers frequently make this mistake. They enjoy the connections with students so much, they don't wish to share that joy with other adults. But youth suffer from this attitude. Youth workers must be in the business of recruiting, training, and keeping great volunteers – not just forming connections with youth themselves, but also connecting youth to other adults who care.

Be careful not to overburden your adult and student leaders by asking them to make friends with new students when their relational capacities are already maximized (that is, all of their connection points are filled). If you do, visitors will have unrealistic expectations that they will have the opportunity to make new friends. Instead, follow the example of one youth group I know: Constantly take in new leaders, and form small groups around them with new students. This way, you'll make the most of everyone's relational potential.

## Recognize Your Teen "Connectors"

Many youth groups include teens whom Malcolm Gladwell identifies as "connectors."[6] They are like the big green or red Lego platforms on which many clusters can be connected. Connectors have membership in several clans, and perhaps even several tribes. Gladwell points out that connectors do not have close friendships in any one group, preferring many casual friendships over a few deep ones. Connectors have well-developed social skills and are respected across tribal lines. They are infectious personalities – their ideas are contagious to those around them. Gladwell believes this type of person can start social "epidemics," spreading new styles or information. These are the Paul Reveres of our youth groups. One connector in my youth group has single-handedly filled several vans for our regular youth events with friends from various clans and tribes. They all now come to our youth group on a regular basis.

As we recognize musical ability, scholastic ability, and athletic ability, we also need to recognize and use the special gifts of connectors, working with them to spread the love of God.

## Respect, Reflect, and Be Real

Great relationships with teenagers have a few requirements.

First, treat your youth with respect. Each one of those connection points is precious. If a teen gives one to you, treat it as a valuable treasure from God. Don't view youth as "yours" because they happen to come to your church or the campus group you coordinate. They are not there to make you look good. In far too many places controlled by adults, teens are treated like objects. Give teens the same signals of respect you would give any other adult: make eye contact, listen to their opinions, ask them meaningful questions. I heard recently of a school principal who knew almost every student by name. She would take time to find out how each of her students was. This wise woman knew the importance of genuine connection with youth, and, with the simplest of cues, let her students know they were important. She was deeply cherished and respected by her students. They will never forget her.

Teens are not little children who need babysitting, nor delinquents who need to be entertained in order to stay out of trouble. They are priceless treasures, blessed by God with talents, desires, and dreams. They are worth so much that the Lord died to win them back. It is an honour and a privilege to have the opportunity to teach them, to have the ability to influence their lives, and to simply enjoy being with them. Humbly recognize that you've been given these awe-inspiring relationships because God also wants *you* to be blessed in the process. So slow down and take the time to really connect with teens.

Second, aim to reflect God in your human connections. Because God is trinity, all that is spiritual is relational. Spirituality is not just about doing religious "stuff," it is about loving people. When we get together in caring communities, modelling our behaviour toward each other after Jesus' example, we mirror God of the trinity. Celebration, forgiveness, prayer, worship, and mystery all find their home in a joyful community. Our worship of God must be more than a set of historical poetry recitals or teens will stampede away. If we have a living, growing relationship with God, teens' interests will be piqued. People who are passionate about God intrigue them.

Third, be real – be yourself. Adolescents pick up the scent of pretenders, teen wannabes, or parents looking for an expanded family. As one youth magazine states, "their BS detectors are always on." Being real is one step more raw than being authentic – think of it as self-honesty on steroids. If you can laugh at yourself, then you're well on your way to being real. A good question to ask yourself is, "Do I like youth?" Do you really like the students, or did somebody volunteer you for the job while you were absent from a meeting? If you are trying to fill a role you hate, get out now. Teens can smell you.

If your passion for this generation is presently tarnished, get away for a day, or a weekend, and ask God to stir your heart again for the teens he has entrusted to your care. The first prayer off the lips of youth workers before the big pizza party or ski trip should be, "God, restore my love for these young people."

## Be an "Aunt" or "Uncle"

The relationships between adult volunteers and teens have a certain flavour of years gone by. Years ago, an extended family of aunts, uncles, and grandparents all had a role in the raising of children. In the old television show *The Waltons*, when John-boy wrecked the car, he knew his dad would yell at him, so he went to talk to his grandpa first. His grandfather was committed to John-boy's well-being, but had emotional distance because he was not John-boy's parent. He could ease the pain of the situation while giving John-boy some ideas on how to approach his father. The concept of an involved extended family now seems to have fallen by the wayside, but youth workers can fulfill the roles of those relations.

Mike Yaconelli, a veteran youth worker for over fifty years, told a story concerning his teenage son. One day his son brought a friend home. Mike started up a conversation with this boy and learned that he had failed French. Falling into his role as a relational youth worker, Mike told the boy that he would get over it, and that he should get a medal for taking French in the first place. As the boys made their way upstairs, Mike heard his son's friend say, "Your dad is so cool." Yet later on, when Mike's son came home and announced that he had failed English, Mike told him, "Get upstairs and study. You're grounded for the week." When questioned on the double standard, Mike replied, "It's different; you're my son."

Parents are emotionally invested in the successes and failures of their children. They have a hard time being dispassionate about major events in their teens' lives. For youth workers, it is different. We also want what is best for our youth, we are also invested in their well-being, but we have the emotional distance to advise them dispassionately, filling much the same role that aunts and uncles filled in the extended families of old.

I have been the first person a pregnant teen talks to. I remove myself from the situation enough to address her emotions and clarify her options. Her parents, when she talks to them, typically get more passionately involved; perhaps some of their own self-worth is tied up in their child.

Whatever the reason, parents are compelled to give direction to their growing children. This is a good thing – teenagers need direction, and their parents are responsible for giving it to them.

We, as youth workers, are not another set of parents for youth. Most of the kids we work with have a parent or even several, and they don't need another one. Some youth workers extend their mothering and fathering instincts into other families' lives. They help teens because of the high they receive from the emotional attachment of parenting, or because they are attempting to make up for past mistakes in their own families. Good youth workers, though, maintain an aunt- or uncle-like emotional separation, allowing parents to parent.

Most teenagers do not form lifelong attachments to us. We are simply helpers on their way, not parental substitutes. Teenagers need to learn to live and make decisions for themselves. As a friend of mine once said, "If your dreams for your youth many years down the road have you in the picture...perhaps your dreams are not big enough!"

## Learn Interpersonal Skills

Educational philosopher Howard Gardner suggests that people have various levels of inter- and intra-personal intelligence. He defines inter-personal intelligence as the ability to understand other people – what motivates them, how they work, how to work in cooperation with them. People with intra-personal intelligence are able to turn inward, to form an accurate model of their inner selves and to use that model to navigate effectively through life.[7] Both kinds of intelligences are needed in youth work.

A key skill for youth workers is the ability to broaden acquaintances and build friendships. We do not ask people to share their deepest, darkest secrets the moment we meet them. Good youth workers start conversations something like this: "Hi my name is _____. I don't think I've met you before. What school do you go to? What are some of the hobbies you're into?" By collecting general information, we often discover common interests, which help us to build friendships. If you don't have a common interest with a teenager, you need to become a student of one of their interests. Once you develop a common interest, those Lego blocks snap together.

When I worked in an economically depressed area of a rundown city, skinny thirteen-year-old Jimmy would come over to my office once in a while. He lived next door. After a while, I could sense that he wanted to be my friend, so I asked some general questions to find out his interests. Learning that he liked skateboarding, I got him to teach me how. After a couple of close brushes with death, I found a safer interest: He collected baseball cards. On occasional Saturday mornings, I would take him to the baseball card shop. I would buy him one pack, and we would trade the few cards I was now collecting. He taught me what to look for in cards – how to keep rookie cards, or those of athletes with great records who were close to retirement.

One day, when Jimmy came to my church office, I was busy and didn't really have the time to talk with him. But before I could cut the conversation short, he told me he heard me talk a lot about God. He wanted a relationship with God like the one I had. Needless to say, I took the time to talk to him.

Ten years after I had left that church, Jimmy wrote me: "Hey, haven't heard from you in a while. Do you still collect baseball cards? I think some may be worth something now. Thought I would send you a note and say thank you for being there for me. I had no dad, and my mom had more boyfriends than I can remember. You were the one person who was there for me through my teen years. Thanks!"

General information leads to common interests. Common interests lead to relationships. Relationships are the base from which change takes place in the lives of teenagers – change that will ripple for generations.

## Form a New Kind of Tribe

People sometimes wrongly conclude that relational ministry is the opposite of programming. Relationships are not just one-on-one; they evolve out of strong communities. Therefore, we need to work on building strong communities as well as strong one-on-one relationships. Sometimes the dynamics of a group are what will draw students who would never be reached and strengthened by individual contact. More than once, parents have asked me if they should force their teens to go to a church youth group. My answer is yes, force them to go three or four times, then give them the freedom to decline. Many students who wouldn't look me in the eye in the church hallway have been won by the fun and the friendliness of the group.

Groups require programming, whether it takes the form of discussion, games, or simply hangout time and location. When we think through our group ministry, we need to figure out how to build a tribe with godly values and activities that build cohesiveness.

The central value of our new tribe must be *agape* love, modelled after Jesus' example of self-sacrificing care of all types of people. Youth workers need to redeem the word "love." We must strip it of all sexual and exploitative innuendo and redefine it. Love is a decision. Love is modelled by adult volunteers who live it in front of teens. It is crucial that those with strong, godly values be the ones who have that influence in the youth group.

If *agape* love is not the central value of your new tribe, then outreach is not taking place. Despite your best intentions, you may be merely providing another venue for deviant behaviour. I have visited too many youth groups in which the values the students are learning are no different from those they have learned from their experiences in a harsh world. But when faithful, spiritual teens set the values of the group, the uninitiated teen is invited to become a part of a counterculture – a place where God's love and acceptance reign.

At retreats, I often ask youth sponsors where they have seen God's work in the previous year. One youth pastor told me about a young girl with a poor self-image. She had allowed people around her to treat her like dirt, because she believed that she was dirt. Then the youth group bought her a new dress. This simple act of kindness not only breathed new life into the young girl, but also enlivened the entire youth group.

Love involves long-term commitment. The troubled youth I've worked with over the years have this in common: Many adults bob in and out of their lives – case workers, lawyers, police, psychologists, teachers. They come, perform their necessary professional role, and go. These youth crave what every youth needs: a place to belong; a place to sink down roots; adults and peers who love them for who they are; a community that says, "You are at home with us." Youth groups can provide caring adults and a place to belong.

It simply comes down to loving youth and committing to the creation of an intergenerational community. The myths and rituals of a tribe are built over time spent together in memory-building activity and in dialogue. At my present church, after every youth meeting we hop into cars and go hang out at a fast-food restaurant. The students love the relational time. Connections between adults and teens are strengthened. I've noticed that most counselling opportunities – and the best spiritual discussions – happen long after the official meeting is over. Simply allow for informal relationship-building times, and large meetings naturally turn into small-group relational events.

An American mega-church conducts a separate service for its younger crowd, with round tables where people sit to discuss the message. Refreshments and prayers for each other are shared between friends. These relational elements draw the young people out and draw them into listening to the good news of Jesus.

Good questions to ask yourself when building your ministry are these: What part of our youth program builds relationships? Are we allowing for memory-making moments? Are groups asked to work together on projects? Do we allow time for friends to sit back and talk and pray?

## Recognize the Importance of Clans

Never underestimate the importance of friendship clans to youth. Hoping to break up cliques, adults often split clans up for games or for bunking on retreats. This practice gives youth, and youth workers, fits. Conflict escalates as the young people try to sneak into groups they really want to be with.

You can work within friendship clans, using their strengths to your advantage. Instead of breaking them up, perhaps invite others who have not yet joined groups to take part. Discussions within clans often continue after the youth group time is over. In our outreach ministry, most of the students are unchurched. We break the group up into their clans for discussion. These teens will discuss spiritual ideas with very little prodding because they are with their friends.

## Create Mentoring Opportunities

What is exciting is that teens are open to relationships with adults. Teenagers' heroes have always been those who are older. As Larry Richards writes, "Simply put, young people respond to adults who help them, and if they are not turned off by a leader's personality or incompetence, will model themselves after him/her."[8] This fact can lead to one of the strongest connecting relationships on the planet – the one between mentor and protégé.

In mentoring's simplest form, adults build strong relationships with one to four young people who are drawn to them by taking personal responsibility for the spiritual growth of the youth. Mentoring is an exchange: teens offer the gift of being open to influence and adults offer the gift of time. Mentoring researcher Laurent A. Daolz described the outcome of mentoring in this way: "As we grow we come to realize that [the mentors'] gift is not the opportunity to become like them but the challenge to become more fully ourselves through them. They call forth the best we have. They invite us to transcend ourselves. They embody our deep aspirations."[9]

Mentoring relationships are valuable tools for every youth worker, no matter what our gifts. As we speak, or organize, or even set up chairs, we are modelling. No other educational form has more transformative power.

A teen named Zach asked me to be his mentor when he was in his final two years of high school. His life was, by his own diagnosis, too busy. I briefly described how I make a time for prayer in my routine and a special place for prayer in my room. I mentioned to him the benefits of quiet time to reflect on the activities of the week. The next Saturday morning, when I went to pick him up, Zach's mother asked me to come in. She gave me a stern look, and asked if I could talk some sense into her boy. "Go up to his room and see what I mean," she told me. As I knocked and entered, I first noticed a pile of clothes, still on their hangers, piled high in the corner. Zach greeted me enthusiastically, saying, "Dave, look what I've done – I've made a prayer corner, too!" There was Zach's former closet, cleared of clothes and set up with a beanbag chair and candles. Many youth, like Zach, want to build close relationships with adults and be influenced in the process.

It is important to realize up front that youth may not intentionally be looking for relationships with youth workers. In our culture, meaningful adult-teen relationships outside of family are rare. One youth told me, "I never realized how good this could be until after we became friends. It just wasn't one of my goals. I never would have thought I could get along with an adult." Despite their countercultural nature, voluntary adult-teen friendships are deeply meaningful and transformative, and they happen when adults make them a priority.

## A Word to Communicators

Our relationships with young people shape even the way we speak to them. Students are much less likely to listen to a teacher or speaker who has not formed a relationship with them, even if the information is good and interesting. Whenever I speak at a youth camp or group, I make it a high priority to spend as much relational time as I can with the group before, during, and after my presentations. For my message to connect with them, they must sense that I genuinely like hanging out with them and have their best interests in mind.

Storytelling is a bridge-builder in relational speaking. When a good storyteller speaks, the heart rates of the listeners increase, they start to sweat, their eyes dilate, their emotions soar. The storyteller and the listeners experience the story together and form a relationship through that experience. Many teens are already walking in a story of their own making; tap into a teen's internal story, and you tap into the inner person.

Through storytelling, it is possible to build relationships even in large-group settings. As I was walked through a crowd of teens at a Christian music festival, one student stopped me and spoke to me as if we were the closest of friends. He brought up a story I had told about rock climbing and laughed about how real it was to him. I smiled, was gracious, and quickly thumbed through my mental Rolodex trying to remember who he was. Finally I gave up and asked where we had met. He replied, "Oh, don't you remember? We were in Albany. We had such a great time!" All of a sudden it dawned on me: This teen was one of a thousand at a speaking venue. To him we were friends because we had gone through the experience of my stories together.

## A Word to Parents

Parents should recognize the good news in all this. Your kids actually want a relationship with you. Teens are not allergic to adults. This fact was a key underlying theme Reg Bibby discovered as he waded through hundreds of informal survey comments. So slow down and take the time to reconnect with your kids.

## Remember: God Is a Relationship, Not an Idea

The importance of relationships affects how we represent God in theology and worship. Young people don't respond to a Jesus exalted high and lifted up as the head of the church. They listen to a Jesus who is mysteriously other, yet stands beside them as a friend and a brother.

Churches that communicate well to the new generation have graciously moved toward an emphasis on the immanence of Jesus, who is Emmanuel, "God with us." Past generations met God through hymns that tended to be more doctrinal and informational (e.g. "A Mighty Fortress Is Our God"). New songs – and old hymns that are still loved, such as "More Love to Thee" and "Be Thou My Vision" – address Jesus as a friend and a lover of our souls. These hymns speak to Jesus directly and are intimate, with lines such as "Let me be a joy to you, O God" or "Open the eyes of my heart, Lord." To help the new generation understand who Christ is, we need to include these relational signs of our faith.

In our millennial culture, young people form diverse tribes and clans. The job before us is to create and recreate tribes apart, in which the law of God's love and the message of hope are the cornerstones of these teens' reality.

## To Do Today

- Write out a prayer and tape it to the side of your night table. Let the prayer be one that reminds you of your daily need: "Lord, restore my love for these young people."
- Who is the most spiritual person you know? Make a point to have coffee with them and ask them to mentor you. You can only take youth where you yourself are being taken.
- Make a list of general questions you can ask new students. Use this list as a reminder for yourself and as a training tool for your volunteers.
- Draw a map of the relationships in your youth group or student club. Who is friends with whom? Who are the connectors? Is anybody left out of friendship groups?
- Give your youth group permission to invite their friends to your next meeting.
- Increase connection points by writing notes by hand to some of your teens. If you work with volunteers, why not catch up over coffee and work together on a note to a teen in your group?
- Give your youth group or club a survey (questions on a scale of 1 to 5) that asks them how much they feel love in the group, how safe they feel sharing personal information with the group, etc.
- Go through your hymnbook and put a check beside all the hymns that address God in a prayer.
- Start a database of your students' interests so you can connect them with others in your group with the same interests. Then make a database of adults who can develop these interests further.

CHAPTER THREE
# Weightless Authority

N ame any teen movie. Do you have it in your head? Who were the "bad guys" or the "town idiots"? Most likely, they were the school principal, a parent, a politician, a priest or pastor. These people have in common a position of power, which they can use to manipulate the outcomes they desire. In most of these movies, the teens win out in the end, gaining freedom from the heavy-handed hierarchy. Teens love to hate certain kinds of authority figures. They dream of a society of weightlessness, where everyone is equal.

## Survey Says: Many Teens Have Lost Respect for Adults and Institutions

Despite being largely segregated in their own tribes, today's teens still interact with adults and authority figures. The PTC surveys have given teens over the years a chance to rate this interaction. The surveys gave teens an opportunity to be on the delivery end of the report card for a change. Here's how adults generally, and institutional leaders specifically, fared.

### Report Card for Adults in General

Adults generally have difficulty relating outside their peer group. Many lack empathy toward teens. Occasionally they manipulate or bully teens to get their own way. They are now treating teens with less dignity than in earlier survey periods. *Disclaimer: These ratings do not apply to parents and many individual adults who continue to make tremendous differences in the lives of the younger generation.*

TABLE 3.1 **Teen Perception of Adult Respect Levels**

"Adults respect young people's opinions."
(% that agreed)

| Year | Agree | Strongly Agree | Total | Grade |
|------|-------|----------------|-------|-------|
| 2000 | 4 | 26 | 30 | F |
| 1987 | 4 | 46 | 50 | D |

*Bibby, PTC 2000, 1984 data sets*


TABLE 3.2 **Teen Perception of Adult Influence Levels**

(% that rated an adult as influencing their lives)

| Type of Adult | A Great Deal | Quite A Bit | Total | Grade |
|---------------|--------------|-------------|-------|-------|
| Mother | 48 | 33 | 81 | A- |
| Father | 35 | 35 | 70 | B- |
| Teachers | 8 | 28 | 36 | F |
| Another adult you respect | 21 | 37 | 58 | D+ |

*Bibby, PTC 2000 data set*

Most teens today believe they are discriminated against because of their age. A common complaint we hear is that, while teens are expected to show respect to adults, that respect is not reciprocated. Since 1984, the number of teens who believe adults do not respect their opinions has increased by 20%! We have to do better. In this chapter we will address the traits of effective adults.

# Report Card for Leaders of Social Institutions: C- to Failure!

We did not find evidence to support claims that youth today are more respectful of institutions than youth of previous eras. The surveys reveal that teens' respect for the leaders of most institutions, such as schools, the police force, the courts, and television, has declined since the mid-1980s. Police and schools are garnering the trust of only about two-thirds of teens. Religious institutions inspire confidence in only 40% of youth. The only institution to have made a noticeable comeback is government, which since 1992 has returned to 1984 numbers.

TABLE 3.3 **Teen Confidence in Leaders**

"How much confidence do you have in the people in charge of..."
% indicating "A Great Deal" or "Quite a Bit"

| Institution | 2000 | 1992 | 1984 | Grade | % Change from 1984-2000 |
|---|---|---|---|---|---|
| Police | 62 | 69 | 77 | C- | -15 |
| School | 63 | 67 | 69 | C- | -6 |
| Court system | 52 | 59 | 67 | D- | -15 |
| Television | 44 | 61 | 57 | F | -13 |
| Provincial government | 41 | 32 | 41 | F | — |
| Federal government | 41 | 27 | 40 | F | +1 |
| Religious organizations | 40 | 39 | 62 | F | -22 |

*Derived from Bibby,* Canada's Teens, *2001: 193*

These figures should concern everyone in society. But note that, despite the downward trend, the picture painted is not completely one of doom and gloom. *Teens today are still just as likely to trust in institutional leadership as to be disenchanted with it.* To paint this generation as deeply disillusioned with the mechanisms of society is to overstate the case.

Leaders of religious groups have suffered the sharpest drop in the level of confidence they inspire. The 22% trust slippage is staggering. Why have we lost the trust of our teens, and how will we regain it? Let us debate this in denominational headquarters, seminaries, churches, and para-church organizations. The task to regain trust will be monumental. Still, there is good news for religious groups. Confidence has stabilized, and even gone up slightly, since 1992. Perhaps teens' negative perceptions of religious leaders bottomed out with the televangelist scandals of the '80s and the clergy sexual-abuse cases of the '90s.

Leaders such as Rev. Dale Lang, whose son Jason was killed by teen violence, have done their part to bolster teen confidence in religious leaders. Dale's inspirational story amidst raw tragedy – the exponential pain of bullying, the power of love, and the personal freedom he has found in Jesus to forgive – has been shared with well over 100,000 students in packed junior and senior high-school auditoriums across Canada. Dale says the most frequent response he gets from administrators is "Our teens have never been more attentive in an assembly." Only time will tell whether Dale's efforts are a temporary blip on a downward trajectory or representative of a new level of visible authenticity among religious leaders.

## Teen Views of God

When looking at teen perceptions of authority figures, we feel we would be remiss if we didn't also address teen perceptions of God and Jesus. The survey asked particularly helpful questions in this area.

TABLE 3.4 **Teen Perceptions of God and the Character of Jesus**

"Do you believe…?"

(% indicating "Yes, I definitely do" or "Yes, I think so")

|  | 2000 | 1992 | 1984 | % Change from from 1984-2000 |
|---|---|---|---|---|
| God exists | 73 | 81 | 85 | -12 |
| God or a higher power cares about you | 67 | — | — | — |
| Jesus was the divine son of God | 64 | — | 85 | -21 |
| You have experienced God's presence | 36 | — | 34 | +2 |

*Bibby, PTC 2000, 1992, 1984 data sets*

Note that nearly three-quarters of the teen population acknowledged God's existence and two-thirds acknowledged Jesus' divinity. Today's teens have not abandoned the supernatural dimensions of Christian perceptions of faith! It is clear that most teens are not mad at God, nor are they afraid to admit their belief in God and Jesus on a survey.

However, belief in both God and the divinity of Jesus has declined significantly since 1984. To our knowledge, these alarming levels are the lowest ever tracked in Canada. Are we finally beginning to observe the result of generations growing up with decreased religious exposure? It appears to be so.

The decrease is not entirely negative for genuine faith groups. As a spiritual director of mine says, "Some views of God have to die – God and Jesus as oppressor have to be abandoned before a correct understanding of the God of love can emerge." And a key finding is that 67% of teens believe that God cares about them. This question was asked for the first time in the 2000 survey, and a staggering two out of every three teens acknowledged belief in a caring deity. Think about it – two-thirds of the youth population believes that God is compassionate! Yet only one in three reported having felt God's presence. Those who *have* personally experienced God have a great opportunity here to assist youth seeking their own experience of God's love. Most teens believe God and Jesus to exist, and believe them to care. This reality is an open ministry door for those who know how to walk through it.

## Today's Teen Ideal: Living Weightless

Imagine a world where everyone carries the same value and every voice is heard. This is the ideal for many in the younger generation. The dream of a weightless society is lived out in on-line fantasy games in which one can lead a war campaign or own local shops in cyberville. These popular on-line games allow youth to live in a world where everyone is treated equally and seriously.

The Internet in general is proving to be a powerful equalizing force. With eBay, we are now experiencing a consumerism in which the customer, rather than the business, sets the price. This retail giant is now worth more than K-mart, Toys "R" Us, Nordstrom, and Saks, combined.[1] Is it possible its success is related to its fulfillment of the next generation's ideal of weightlessness?

While the removal of all hierarchies in business – and in life in general – may be an unreachable goal, the movement toward more equitable communities is a powerful drive within adolescents. Whether such an ideal is reachable or not, teens see weightlessness as possible, and so judge much of their experience by the equity of the situation. If we are to reach teenagers, we must address their desire for a level playing field.

# Why Is This the Case?

It is difficult to understand an ongoing decrease in confidence in institutional respect and loyalty. There is likely no single factor. Fragmentation, education, media, philosophy, and psychology may each have played a role. Certainly, each feeds off the others in the formation of public opinions.

## Fragmentation's Role

Nothing stays the same for long these days. Television channels multiply faster than rabbits. Clothing styles will have changed again by the time you finish this chapter. New businesses (some run by teens' classmates) open every month and others close down. For some, even family is now an ever-changing kaleidoscope of people clusters. As one teen puts it, "Every Christmas I am reminded why I only see my relatives once a year." All this instability has given teens the sense that everything is in flux – there are no hierarchies, nothing that is permanent. Authority figures come and go. Institutions reinvent themselves. What can teens put their trust in? Trust is built slowly, over time; these days, few things – or even people – are around for long enough to gain a teen's trust.

## Education's Role

Generations ago, the Nuremberg war trials were the current event. Almost every school child was asked to write an essay on why leaders should not be obeyed if they ask you to do something morally wrong. A whole generation stood in judgment of the Nazis, some of whom performed horrible acts "because they were told to do so." Never again – the spell of the "goodness" of those in charge was broken. Respect for authority declined, and has been declining ever since.

## Media's Role

Over the years, that spell would be broken again and again as the news media fed us the spectacular and the horrifying. News story by news story, we came to understand that institutions were stained through with evil. Government officials were receiving kickbacks and religious officials were having affairs. The names Jim Bakker and Jimmy Swaggart lowered an entire generation's expectation of religious institutions. The collective myth of the modern age whispered that institutions are somehow corrupting – if you become associated with one, the stain transfers to you. Media now routinely degrade parents, ministers, and governments. We have lost the very concept of reverence. No one and nothing is special or sacred.

## Philosophy's Role

Behaviourists initially believed that power meant getting someone to do something that they did not want to do.[2] Through reward and punishment, people could be controlled. This belief was challenged by a group of late-twentieth-century philosophers some call the Realists.[3] People like Bhaskar and Giddens understood power to reside in the structure of relationships and not in specific events.[4] Using the analogy that copper conducts electricity because of its structure,[5] they argued that power is conducted through societal structure. For example, police officers have the power to make an arrest because they have a socially structured role. Teachers have the power to mark papers and send students to the principal's office because of their socially structured roles.

The Realists' view of power is now in vogue in North America. When things go wrong, it is quite often structure that is blamed by the media. If someone makes a mistake at a water treatment plant, it's because the government did not set up adequate guidelines, not because a person was negligent. If a man commits a murder, it is because he has a traumatic family history or did not have access to government programs. If power lies within structures rather than individuals, so does responsibility.

In previous generations, many institutions were seen as above criticism. But with philosophy emphasizing the power within systems, institutions now shoulder much of the responsibility for society's problems. People in positions of power are now in the public eye, and need to be much more careful about how they use their power. Unfortunately, this much-needed rethinking of power has also lowered a generation's trust in institutions, and has displaced the responsibility for many problems from individuals onto institutions.

## Psychology's role

In the teen years, children acquire new mental capacities that improve their ability to judge. Jean Piaget observed that children below the age of eleven or twelve are likely to think on a concrete level, mentally manipulating things in their heads they have already experienced with their hands.[6] Once, in a Grade 4 "kids' club" class I was teaching, I asked the students for a definition of "love." The children gave me concrete examples: baking cookies for a grandparent, not punching someone who spilled Sprite on them. Their concept of love was limited to concrete events they had personally experienced.

But by the teen years, students think in abstractions and ideals. I met Susan at a country church in western New York. She was in Grade 6 and had a razor-sharp mind. She would shoot her hand up to answer every question I asked. She led every class in the most "stars on the wall" for attendance and memorized verses. I left that church and came back four years later to visit. I met a very different Susan on the streets. She wore the dark eyes of someone who had lived too long. Her head was half shaved, and she was pregnant with an older man's child. I approached her and tried to renew a dusty relationship. She was genuinely happy to see me. During our conversation, I asked her if she still hung out at the church. She said, "No way!" She told me she had questions no one could answer, like "If there is a God, why do bad things happen to good people?" Because no one in the church had an answer, she "chucked the faith."

Once ideals can be conceptualized, they can be applied. Teens, for example, can now imagine an ideal family, and some come to the painful awareness that they do not belong to one (see Table 3.5). Or they might have grown up in a poor family, never realizing they were poor. Never realizing, that is, until they were teenagers.

TABLE 3.5 **Teens Who Want a Home Like the One They Grew Up In**

| |
|---|
| All teens — 71% |
| Teens whose parents live together — 75% |
| Teens from single-parent homes — 60% |
| Teens whose biological parent lives with a partner — 50% |

*Bibby, PTC 2000 data set*

Teens can now imagine ideal governments, ideal churches, ideal schools. The teenager is staggered by the silliness of structures that waste resources, practise inequities, or teach useless knowledge. Any institution is fair game, but the church in particular is a neon target that draws continual flaming arrows of disapproval. Many teens feel that they know just as much as anyone else, and that if their reflective abilities are not recognized, they are being treated like children.

# What Does This Mean for Youth Work?

In working with teens, we must lay down any lust for power. We must not seek to manipulate and domineer. That kind of abuse is an act of treason against the God in whose image youth are made.[7] We are already at a disadvantage in how teens perceive us if we are physically larger than they are, if we use fancy words when we speak to them, or if we make teens use our titles when speaking to us. These symbols of our power over them inhibit them from reaching Christ through us.

## Empathize with Teens' Feelings of Powerlessness

Power issues are important when working with adolescents. Most adolescents feel powerlessness. They tend to be stereotyped. They are no longer children, but cannot yet claim the positions of power reserved for adults. Adolescents find themselves on a difficult middle ground where they are often seen as problematic or, at best, ignorable. For example, if a group of adults and adolescents are interacting at a fast food establishment, adolescents will inevitably be blamed for any excessive noise or spilt drinks, regardless of who is responsible. I once walked into a school gym to retrieve some material left behind from a youth event. The custodian mistook me for a teenager and yelled at me for being there. When he discovered I was an adult who was renting their facility, he apologized. Many adolescents have first-hand and frequent experience of this "yell first, ask questions later" attitude.

## Give Teens Dignity

When I speak to groups of adolescents, adult sponsors or parents are often a part of the meeting. These adults walk into a room filled with teenagers and move past them to introduce themselves to adults on the other side of the room. It's as if the teens are non-persons. Are these adults afraid of adolescents, or do they just feel that the teens don't matter? I enjoy entering a room filled with students and adults and talking to several groups of adolescents before I talk to the adults. The youth usually react with surprise, genuine openness, and smiles when they realize I am treating them as equals.

When I asked a group of teenagers who their favourite teachers were, they did not choose the funniest or most skilled teacher, but the ones that treated them with dignity and respect. They reacted with comments such as, "She treats me like an adult," "He takes me seriously," "She actually learned something from me!" While I was completing my master's degree, I worked as a teaching assistant. As providence would have it, I was assigned to assist one of the most phenomenal instructors on campus. This professor was inspiring. She was passionate about life, competent in her subject matter, and best of all she delighted in her students. She'd roam the entire room enthusiastically interacting with the class, and by the end of the semester was using everyone's first name...in a class of 160! But the full magnitude of this professor's impact didn't hit me until one student made a casual remark I will never forget. During a visit to my office, the student confided, "When Dr. ____ uses my first name, this place turns from black-and-white to colour." In our increasingly bureaucratic and impersonal world, there is great joy in being known and treated with dignity. When people in positions of authority figure this out, the younger generation comes alive.

## Create Weightless Authority

Treat teenagers as equals. Our theology certainly asks that of us. Teenagers are our joint heirs in Christ. Allow the names of some of the great teenagers of the Bible to inspire you: David in the face of Goliath, Mary listening to the angel, Jeremiah receiving his call, Joseph receiving his dreams. Teens are no less children of God than we are. In fact, God may be moving a world through them.

A zero-gravity atmosphere occurs in a youth group when teens see us, not as people in positions of power, but as equals. It is created when we stop and listen to our teens' concerns, when we answer their questions thoughtfully, after communicating to them that their thoughts and feelings are significant.

## Treat Opportunities to Influence as Gifts

I often hear adults say they need to gain teens' respect. "If I am not respected, then the kids won't do what I ask them," they worry. There are times when we youth workers must ask our teens to do things they don't want to do or set guidelines they don't want to follow: that on a retreat, guys don't go in the girls' cabins, and curfew is 1:00 a.m., for example. But power doesn't necessarily mean control over someone else. John French and Bertram Raven described a kind of power that is as gift given from one person to another: the power to influence.[8] They call this type of power "referent power." It is seen not as a power over another person but a power with them. Teens give adults the power to influence because we are important people in their lives – because we have established relationships with them. The adult becomes their reference.

The gift of influence can only be given. It cannot be demanded. It is a holy gift, an invitation to an inner life. Teenagers give this gift of power to those they respect, to those who treat them as equals. The heroes on the posters that hang on teens' walls have not demanded power, but won it, through relational cues.

## Be Fully Present

Too often I have seen youth workers say hello to every passer-by when a teen is talking to them. The message they communicated is, "I am only half listening to you, because you are not as super-important as I am." Or, "...you are not as important as the person passing by." Eye contact and real absorption in what someone is saying is the meat of real dialogue.

Adolescents are self-sensitive. You will not gain their respect until they feel you care about what they have to say.

The philosopher Nicholas Burbules, describing a relational dialogue, writes, "We follow what our partners in dialogue are trying to say, we think along with them, we try to imagine matters from their point of view, to a degree that we do not bother with in ordinary speech."[9] We must empty ourselves of our concerns before we can give others' concerns central importance. No wonder Philippians, chapter two, in the New Testament speaks of Christ's emptying of self in the context of the command to "consider others as better than yourselves."

## Build Trust over the Long Haul

We cannot pretend we are above our students or we will not have any ministry with them. Unfortunately, in some ways power is inherent in who we are as youth workers. We have the power of age, we have the power of being "in charge" of certain events, we have the power of structure in that we are a part of a church or a group. If we happen to be a pastor, we have the power of a title. We are going at the plate with two strikes against us, and the third ball is in the air!

In past generations, a pastor was trusted until proven untrustworthy; now a pastor is not trusted until proven trustworthy. This is particularly true in churches where there is a high turnover of youth pastors. Students will not even begin to give the gift of trust until a youth pastor has stayed at least a year. Those in the later grades may not bother ever to give trust to a new youth pastor again. Youth workers are now forming a movement that, if successful, will allow them to see a group through a four-year cycle of students. We applaud this movement and plead with the churches and para-church organizations to make it emotionally and financially possible for youth workers (paid and volunteer) to have longer ministries.

We often think that schools have far more influence than the church. We have students once or twice a week; the schools have them five days a week. Yet we have a greater longevity than we realize. Schoolteachers get a new class every year. People in the church can influence over a period of several years or even a lifetime.

I witnessed a holy moment at one church-wide retreat. We held an encouragement circle, in which each person had a turn to remain quiet and receive encouragement from the rest of the group. Ken, a farmer in his forties, was in the hot seat, and a sixteen-year-old spoke up to encourage him. His words went something like this: "Hey, Ken, you know all those Sunday school classes you did with me those years? Well, they changed my life. It was great to have someone with me for so long who knew what I was going through."

## Take Student Leadership Seriously

At the first church I was worked in, I held a big youth event and asked two girls to relate their recent practice of spiritual discipline. They got up on stage and giggled and stumbled over what to say as they attempted to communicate their habit of meeting with God in a time of quiet. I was tearing my hair out in the back corner of the room. Would anyone understand what they were talking about? The two didn't make a lot of sense and didn't seem to take it very seriously. But when the meeting was over, several teen girls came up to me to ask if they could form a small group. I wondered what part of my talk had inspired this desire to move forward. Imagine my surprise when they told me that because those two girls had the guts to get up in front of others to talk about their faith, they were inspired to get serious about their faith. By the way, they wanted those two girls to lead their small group. I learned in that meeting that the power of the peer is greater than any college degree I could wave.

We must come up with better ways to involve students in leadership. But just having them in leadership is not the full answer. I find that most youth groups who have student leaders vote them into the positions. Although that sounds democratic and equitable, it is often the popular and the outgoing who are chosen.

Jesus-style leadership is open to all who are willing to serve. In our outreach ministries, we have an open group of leaders. Admission into the leadership team is not achieved through a vote, but through the possession of the qualities of faithfulness, availability, and a teachable spirit. Anyone is welcome, as long as they are able to assume responsibilities, attend all leadership meetings, and lead Bible studies and prayer for the group. Newcomers fit in quickly when they are encouraged to do things that don't take much experience, such as taking pictures, writing letters, and exchanging encouragement cards. The route to increased attendance in your youth group might be through the door of service.

Youth leaders need to challenge teen leaders to work with all their heart. The mercy of Christ is not an allowance for mediocrity. Working with Christ to help others requires diligence. Far too often we invite teens to leadership, but give them no challenge – and then wonder why they stay away in droves.

## Build Group Loyalty

Because of the ever-changing world around us, the loyalty of teens to a particular church group is practically as short as their attention span. Twenty years ago, my youth group had a certain pride in their church and their youth group. It was a part of their identity to be from "West Sommerset" and not from "Newfane." Now groups travel with their cluster of friends to the newest and the best. Teens' real loyalty lies with their friends, in part because fewer youth have family connections to the church. The result is church polygamy. A town with eight churches, each with a youth ministry of twenty students, may only have forty teens involved in the church life of the town, not 160! This fact takes some getting used to for those of us concerned with the health of the parish. How do we convey both a healthy acceptance of the broader body of Christ and the advantages to real involvement in a local body? What are the advantages of being a member of a local body of Christ? Here are some suggestions:

### Provide Stability and Security with Intergenerational Leisure Time

Make youth feel wanted and significant by making family-like connections. At our church we hold a free meal for young adults every second Sunday during the school year, and invite the students from the college residence across the street. We encourage adults and families to get involved in the meal preparation and to mingle with the students. Many significant bonds are formed, and numbers of residence students make our church their home away from home. Encourage adult families to take a special interest in specific individuals, or groups of teens or young adults, and go deep in their relationships – even to the degree of informally "adopting" youth into their extended family circles and creating memories together.

### Keep Your Services Fresh and Creative

If two of our services have the same order, similar songs, no surprises, and no change, the students I minister with will tell me we are in a rut. Rituals give a sense of comfort, of being at home. But creativity keeps us awake. We need both in our services. If I change too much, even the young people feel ill at ease. However, if there are no surprises, they leave in packs. As a pastor, I have both the problem and the privilege of being a lightning rod for how the service goes. I sometimes run out of ideas, or try one out that should have been left in my mental closet. To help with this, I have built around me a creativity team. I sit down with my team and explain my sermon. Team members brainstorm with me on ways to bring out the important concepts through drama, visuals, sound bites. They help me see what ideas to leave behind. The students love this weightless environment of open-ended creation.

In conclusion, remember this. Your power as a youth worker is not in your position or title, but in your relationships with youth. By your actions, you either build relational capital or fritter it away. Do your part to offer long-term friendship, wise insight, and creative input in the lives of teens, but know that your relationship with them is gift, wrapped with love and respect.

## To Do Today

- Phone up one of your students (Yes, put this book down and do it now!) and ask them to give a life story (what God has done for them lately) at your next youth meeting. Videotape it if they are too shy to talk in front of others.
- Write down a time when you will start a youth leadership team. Warn your students ahead of time, tell them the requirements, and, in addition to the general call, invite those who you think will be ready to help out.
- Ask five people in your church (they don't have to be on the youth team) to help you dream up creative ways to keep youth meetings fresh. Brainstorm various methods of delivery (videos, dramas, active learning). Give your team an outline of your topic and let them go wild flinging out ideas on how to make it come alive.
- Start debates in your local faith community on subjects such as "Why have we lost the trust of our youth?" and "What steps are we taking to gain that trust back?"
- Take a survey: Ask your teens to list what youth groups they go to, and what is the best part of each.
- Give a workshop for your leaders on listening skills and ways to remember names.
- Walk through your church building with your students and ask them to point out things that represent power to them.
- Have a Bible study with your students in which you chase the use of the word "authority" through the book of Matthew. Discuss the various meanings of the word in this gospel.

CHAPTER FOUR

# Cocoon-Ripping Freedom

T he holiday weekend retreat was awesome! We flung down a zip line, crashed at high speeds while being pulled on a banana tube behind a ski boat, and stayed up late into the night conversing. During the ride home, which is typically rather "blue," we stopped by McDonalds and, as the kids quietly nursed their Cokes, I asked, "Why do we love retreats so much?" The question injected some life into the creeping tide of depression. Several of the kids interrupted me and each other trying to get their explanations out. One student told me, "Retreats and youth group are the only times I can really be myself. I can do what I want to. There are no pressures. I feel so...so free."

## Survey Says: Teens Love Their Freedom

TABLE 4.1 **Love of Freedom**

- 85% of females and 84% of males view freedom as "very important."
- 79% of females and 73% of males view having choices as "very important."

| TOP FIVE MALE TEEN VALUES | TOP FIVE FEMALE TEEN VALUES |
|---|---|
| #1. Freedom | #1. Friendship |
| #2. Friendships | #2. Being loved |
| #3. Having choices | #3. Freedom |
| #4. A comfortable life | #4. Having choices |
| #5. Success | #5. A comfortable life |

*Derived from Bibby,* Canada's Teens, *2001: 13*

Almost every youth places a premium value on freedom and the ability to make personal choices. Gender differences are slight, although males tend to hold freedom slightly higher than relationships, while females do not. The teen love affair with freedom extends to all, regardless of religious or regional affiliations.

TABLE 4.2 **Freedom by Religion and Region**

| |
|---|
| • 84% of Catholics, 81% of Protestants, 87% of teens from other faiths, and 87% of teens with no religious affiliation view freedom as "very important." |
| • 84% of teens from British Columbia, 86% of teens from the prairie provinces, 85% of teens from Ontario, 82% of teens from Quebec, and 90% of teens from the Maritime provinces view freedom as "very important." |

*Bibby, PTC 2000 data set*

Freedom is expressed in a variety of behaviours and attitudes. Teens want freedom – to create, to choose, to experiment, to fuse in new ways, to come as they are. Teens' bodies are their own properties, and they desire the freedom to pierce or tattoo. Whenever I think I have seen every hairstyle and colour, the teens come up with a different mix.

TABLE 4.3 **Expressions of Freedom**

| |
|---|
| • 19% of females and 6% of males have body piercings other than earrings. |
| • 10% of females and 7% of males have permanent tattoos. |
| • 48% of females and 58% of males use alcohol every month or more frequently. |
| • 17% of females and 30% of males use marijuana or hashish every month or more frequently. |
| • 45% of females and 66% of males approve of teens age 15-17 having sex. |
| • 76% of females and 74% of males disapprove of a curfew for teens in their hometown. |

*Bibby, PTC 2000 data set*

For many, the Internet provides freedom of speech, freedom from supervision. So many movies, from cartoons to violent epics, have freedom as their central theme. Teens can travel the globe and talk to anyone, wearing a cyber-face of whoever they want to be. Popular computer games give entrance into a fantasy world, often with no story line, where you are free to do anything you want. A quiet and kind teen in our church becomes a warrior at night, travelling to various cities slicing and dicing anyone who stands in his way.

This love affair with freedom has touched every teen in some way. They fly through the air on skateboards, cut new trails with snowboards, play by their own rules. To many a teen the "no skateboarding" sign in a parking lot is simply another example of the adult conspiracy to stop freedom.

Yet, inevitably, teens' freedom drive leads to concerns among the older generation. Parents, in particular, are prone to question the choices of their sons and daughters.

TABLE 4.4 **Areas of Disagreement Between Parents and Teens**

"Disagreements involve…"
(% indicating "Fairly Often" or "Very Often")

| Area of disagreement | Males | Females |
| --- | --- | --- |
| Jobs around the house | 56 | 60 |
| School | 61 | 49 |
| Concern about safety (driving, etc.) | 52 | 46 |
| Money | 41 | 37 |
| The time teens come in at night | 39 | 40 |
| Concern about staying out of trouble | 40 | 32 |
| Teens' choice of friends | 25 | 25 |
| Concern about drinking | 26 | 20 |
| Concern about dating partners | 17 | 25 |
| Concern about drugs | 24 | 16 |
| Concern about appearance | 20 | 20 |
| Concern about sex | 19 | 17 |

*Bibby,* Canada's Teens, *2001: 64*

## Loving the Spontaneous

The teen love of freedom is a love for the spontaneous. Fine, stable, even boring adults were often spontaneous teens. When one of the students in our youth group had his truck in the shop, he used an insurance-sponsored rental car and discovered that it had, for some insane reason, unlimited mileage. With great joy, he drove from friend's house to friend's house to see who would come with him on a road trip, that night, to Nashville, Tennessee – a fifteen-hour drive away! He arrived at my door at 11:00 p.m., to tell me that a carload of his friends was heading down to Nashville to spend the next day and then come back. He wanted to know if I would come along. When I responded, "I don't think I'll join you this time," they shouted their goodbyes and spun out of the driveway. My wife asked, "Who was that, dear?" "I don't think you want to know," I replied. Adult years tend to dampen our enthusiasm for the spontaneous.

Spontaneity in youth groups is the spice that keeps things interesting. Even in so-called contemporary services, students get bored with the predictable. Our creative team injects spontaneity into our services. In one case, the lights were turned off and spotlights panned across the people, while *Mission: Impossible* music played. Designated students ran out and picked out random people, who were brought onstage and given chocolate bars. The lights went back up, the service continued, and the teens whispered, "Whoa!"

## Freedom from Responsibilities

Many adolescents want to be able to do whatever they want, without cost. They want to be free from rules, and free from other people's expectations. The emotional, addictive, or physical costs that come with some actions are initially unseen. But these forays into freedom can leave scars and do not necessarily prove satisfying over the long run.

TABLE 4.5 **Teen Emotional Scars**

| |
| --- |
| • 46% of teens have a close friend with a severe drug or alcohol problem. |
| • 48% of teens have a close friend who has been seriously depressed. |
| • 43% of teens wonder about the purpose of life "a great deal" or quite a bit." |
| • 42% of teens are bothered "a great deal" or "quite a bit" by boredom. |

*Bibby, PTC 2000 data set*

The desire for freedom stretches into the extended adolescence of college days.[1] College students, however, have many more opportunities to do whatever they want. From the philosophical freedom to experiment with ideas to the moral freedom to experiment with new values and behaviours, the extended adolescents of the college dorm often overdose on "freedom." The sense of breaking away from childhood restrictions is intoxicating. The new independence gives the illusion of freedom without responsibility.[2]

Interestingly, this love of freedom crashes headlong into a relational desire for intimacy. Deep relationships call out for responsibility to one another, which at times restricts freedom. Much of the anxiety of college relationships revolves around this tension between the desire for freedom and the desire for intimacy. Many college students have not yet learned that most of life is meant to be lived in interdependent relationships. In marriage and employment, you cannot "do anything you want, without cost."

# Why Is This the Case?

As a caterpillar breaks free from its cocoon to become a butterfly, so teenagers break free from their childhood homes. They can hardly wait to try their wings of freedom. No longer "controllable," they experiment with new movements and new identities. Many parents, feeling that too much is happening too soon, irrationally try to stuff their emerging adults back into their cocoons. These parents do not properly understand adolescence.

## Understanding Adolescence as Transition

Adolescence is a time of transition from dependent childhood, where one's sense of self is largely shaped by family interaction and values, to independent adulthood, where one sets one's own goals, values, and sense of self. In other words, in adolescence a person develops autonomy and self-direction. Teens need to answer for themselves the life-transforming question "Who am I?" It is a natural part of the teen years to self-evaluate.

Peers, employers, teachers, and adult friends and mentors play a strategic role during this "second individuation."[3] In order to establish identity, teens need separation from their parents. But the data clearly show that many wise moms and dads manage to play a significant role during the teen years by moving from roles as authority figures to new roles as friends, counsellors, and mentors. Most teens appreciate this.

Even teens from solid homes need to explore. New activities are begun. Values, attitudes, behaviours are tried on for size. Many teenagers believe that who they will be in the future is not bounded by the past in any way. As Erik Erikson writes,

> A youth, therefore, is sensitive to any suggestion that it may be hopelessly determined by what went before in life histories or in history. Psychosocially speaking, this would mean that irreversible childhood identifications would deprive an individual of an identity of his own.... For these reasons, a youth often rejects parents and authorities and wishes to belittle them as inconsequential, for it is in search of individuals and movements who claim, or seem to claim, that they can predict what is irreversible, thus getting ahead of the future – which means reversing it.[4]

Peers in informal friendship clans and significant adults model desired dress, language, values, and worldview. These models also become the meters of acceptance that teens observe so closely during their self-exploration. In the process, lessons and skills learned in childhood are massaged, and take on different shapes. New identities are embraced. While some old identities are maintained, others are discarded. Wings develop! An adult with a new configuration of competencies and attitudes emerges.

## Threats to Emergence

Two serious threats to responsible adulthood that teens face during this time are family resistance and peer group deficiencies.

A family resistant to emergence can tragically clip the aspirations of their emerging adult. Resistance often happens because parents are suspicious of the social mores of teen culture – or perhaps society in general – or because they lack understanding of the maturation process. But when they meet with resistance, teens instinctively challenge the threat to freedom by overt or covert rebellion. Teens go their own way, and relationships with their parents fracture. As Josh McDowell says, "rules without relationship equals rebellion."[5] In *Reviving Ophelia*, Mary Pipher warns of two mistakes parents can make: being too authoritarian, or being too lax.[6] Somewhere in the middle lies firmness coupled with respect for the child. Parents often ignore the biblical admonition not to exasperate, embitter, or discourage your children (Eph 6:4; Col 3:21). If family pressure is strong, some teens quietly stay at their parents' side, withdrawing from broader society. They have internalized their parents' fears and, sadly, prefer to stay in the cocoon.

Irresponsible role models can also wreak tragic results. For some youth, the peer group becomes an intense place of conformity. Few things are as potentially devastating in the minds of teens as being shunned from the one group that may accept them. To avoid this, they may take on values that go against their upbringing. I had an interview with an adult who wished to become involved in our church. He told me that during his teen years none of the good kids liked him, so he joined up with the bad kids. In the sweet-smelling air of acceptance, he took on their values. By his own admission, he has been paying for that ever since.

## Missing Rites of Passage

I had lunch one day with a twenty-four-year-old who had just asked a young woman to marry him. That week they were starting to look for a house together. As we talked, he had a dazed look on his face. "I think somewhere along the line I became an adult," he said. "I don't know how. I think it just snuck up on me."

Many pre-modern cultures had rituals that ushered their emerging adults into the culture of adulthood. The initiation rites of some cultures could take days or only moments, but afterwards the youth would have all the privileges and responsibilities of an adult. Youth looked forward to the day they would become adults, when they would move from working hard for their family of origin toward establishing their own family.

What cultural initiation rites does a modern North American child go through to become an adult? The Jewish bar/bat mitzvah and in some places the Catholic confirmation are intended to be adult initiation rites. Yet in modern North America, little is truly gained from these rites as far as adult status is concerned. In fact, many priests complain that confirmation is more often regarded as a graduation from the religious community than a graduation to adulthood. If places of religion do not service the culture at large with initiation rites into adulthood, what does?

Getting a driver's licence or a diploma from high school could be regarded as initiation rites, but do they really afford the respect and position of becoming an "adult" in our society? There are adults who do not drive or have not graduated from high school. Some might argue that marriage or a career commitment is the initiation rite into adulthood for the North American. If so, how can this be a defining ritual when the average age of marriage is being delayed until later in life – if it takes place at all?[7] Career commitments are also occurring much later in life – if at all.[8]

In our modern urban settings we have no meaningful ritual "fires" of transition, so we end up with a generation that sings and dances around transition for many, many years. In fact, many profit companies create artificial "fires of transition" to take advantage of this generation.

Many adults pine for the time when they were free-spirited adolescents. In some ways, we worship youth in our culture. David Elkind observes many "vanishing markers" of adult culture.[9] Adults dress like teens, enjoy the same activities as teens, and long for those days of less responsibility. For the first time in history, five generations are all trying to be young.[10] Richard Foster notes the stress that this creates: "What a terrible burden we place upon ourselves and others in our desperate attempt to stay young. People are in misery because they are not yet twenty-one, and people are in misery because they are past twenty-one, and that leaves most of us in misery most of the time."[11]

Because of this focus on youth, we place less responsibility on our elderly. We push them to the fringes of society instead of revering them for the contributions they have made and significant wisdom they can still contribute. As a result, our seniors have the sense that the young want nothing to do with them. Yet when I give seminars to college students on mentoring relationships, their number-one question after a session is, "How can I find a mentor? The older folks don't seem to want to build relationships with us." The mutual assumption of lack of interest is creating a gulf between the generations.

We need to get in tune with the God-given cycles of life, and stop abandoning teens to the frustrating experience of figuring out adulthood for themselves. In the eyes of teenagers, adulthood is inevitable but, because of its responsibilities, not particularly desired. And their childhood now seems unreal to them. So what do teens have? They are in limbo. The spontaneous, the experience of now, is all they can be sure of. With few cultural markers or rituals to give children the cues that they are now adults, adolescence becomes prolonged. In so-called primitive societies, people in their teen years are expected to be active in exercising the privileges and responsibilities of an adult life. We may bristle at the young ages at which girls get married or boys start jobs in these cultures. But in our culture we wait perhaps too long.

Urbanization is one culprit. As recently as the 1930s, most North American families lived in rural areas, and significant work responsibilities and privileges were given to people in their teen years. Young people would be responsible for driving a tractor long before they could drive a car. Families worked together to fulfill business obligations, complete chores, and produce food.

These days, most North Americans live in urban or suburban settings, and significant work is kept separate from home life. Food production and business are conducted away from the home, and adolescents are not truly needed to help keep the family running. Those in their teens and early twenties are expected to finish high school, and college or university, and only then enter the workforce.[12]

# What Does This Mean for Youth Work?

## Celebrate Adulthood by Incorporating Initiation Rites

Youth workers can shorten the period of adolescent limbo for teens by working closely with parents and communities to incorporate adult initiation rituals. Make it a point for whole communities to celebrate youth transitions such as confirmations or adult baptisms, first jobs, driver's licences, graduations, engagements, and marriages. Or make up an initiation rite, a party for sixteen-year-olds, for example. Whatever the rite, it will be meaningful if it symbolizes the youth's graduation into full adulthood, with a significant voice and responsibilities in the community.

## Model the Joys of Adulthood

There is a freedom and joy that come from the connections we make in adulthood. When your spouse spontaneously says, "I love you," when your children want you present at their soccer games, when your boss thanks you for your reliability, when the youth you mentor lets you know he wants to follow in your footsteps – this is true exhilaration! Youth (and adults) need to be taught to consciously reject the cultural drive for youthfulness by joyfully embracing responsibilities and the non-tangible perks that come with adulthood.

Catholic theologian Henri Nouwen makes this point eloquently in *The Return of the Prodigal Son*:

> Isn't there a subtle pressure in both the Church and society to remain a dependent child? Hasn't the Church in the past stressed obedience in a fashion that made it hard to claim spiritual fatherhood, and hasn't our consumer society encouraged us to indulge in childish gratifications? Perhaps the most radical statement Jesus ever made is: "Be compassionate as your Father is compassionate." God's compassion [as] described by Jesus...invite[s] me to become like God and to show the same compassion to others as he is showing to me.[13]

## Model Appreciation for the Elderly

Responsible adulthood rejects the notion that seniors are disposable and instead celebrates the elderly. There are many opportunities to connect with, learn from, minister beside, and serve the elderly. Seniors and teens can work side by side on projects. Teens can serve shut-ins or offer programs in seniors' centres. Youth groups can invite a pioneer to discuss life during the Depression or a veteran to address the harsh realities of coming of age during the Second World War. The elderly bring a much-needed perspective to youth who are sadly cut off from the past by a candy-coated, short-sighted consumer culture.

## Model the Benefits of Intergenerational Relationships

Most of the small groups in my church are intergenerational. At prayer time, a student will ask for prayer for a history test, and the person beside him will ask for a prayer as she retires from work. Adults and teens connect when neither side expects to be served, but all are ready to roll up their sleeves. In this way, relationships are built.

A few years ago, a youth minister I know and his wife were going through a difficult time in their marriage and ministry. Still, the students they worked with wanted to hang out with them. One night a week the minister opened his home to young adults from the college where he ministered. He told the young people that he and his wife were too broken to lead them but, if they wanted, they could come anyway, and they would care for and pray for each other. Everyone loved the experience, and significant encouragement happened for all present. (I'm happy to report that the minister and his wife worked out their problems and are presently deeply enjoying ministry and life together. Yet they look back with fond memories to the students who tenderly journeyed with them through that dark time.)

## Provide an Understanding of Real Freedom

As students rip free from childhood, we in the Christian community need to provide adult models that give them an understanding of real, healthy freedom.

### Real Freedom Happens in Relationships

During a conversation with Vancouver theologian Rick Watts, I realized that even though relationships and freedom appear to conflict, they do not. Jesus invites us into community, but at the same time it frees us from stifling relationships. Jesus grounds our individual dignity, giving us an identity in relationship to God. The community doesn't determine us; rather, as we gather around God, we mutually celebrate individual expression. Teens, like all of us, need a group to belong to, but one that won't quash their unique identities.

## All Real Freedoms Have Price Tags

Teens are looking for the happiness that freedom can bring. However, youth need help understanding that all freedoms have price tags of responsibilities attached to them. A driver's licence may give you freedom to travel farther, but it comes with the responsibilities of safety to self and others and the cost of maintenance and gas. With the freedom to vote comes the responsibility to examine the issues before voting.

If we do wrong, any freedom we achieve is a false one. One of the price tags attached to every wrong is the further addiction to that wrong. I have just spent some time with a nineteen-year-old who went wild on the "freedom" of getting drunk. When she complained to me that she had to eat certain foods and take iron shots every two days, I asked her why. Her embarrassed reply was that she'd had a short stay in a detox centre, and they were trying to get her body back on track. Addiction is enslavement.

Jesus died to set us free from the slavery of sin. Teens need to learn that we can lean on his power to break free from the addictions of substance abuse, consumerism, lust, backstabbing and gossip, and other sins. As in other forms of emancipation, the first message imprisoned teens need to hear is "You are enslaved." Many teenagers believe they are chasing after freedom, when they are really hammering out links to the chains of slavery.

## Real Freedom is Being Who You Were Made to Be

I have a beautiful custom Guild guitar. It is mine, so I am free to play baseball with it if I want to; however, I am not free from the consequences to my guitar were I to do so. My guitar was created to play beautiful music: blues, alternative, straight-up rock-and-roll. There is a lot of room to experiment and compose with my guitar within the boundaries of music. Playing baseball, though, lies outside the boundaries of music, and it would destroy my guitar to use it for that purpose. Similarly, we are beautiful instruments of God, created in God's image. God has given us personalities, gifts, and futures laced with hope, meaning, and love. Real freedom lies in recognizing and accepting our boundaries, while exploring and celebrating the possibilities within them.

C. S. Lewis puts it another way:

A car is made to run on petrol, and it would not run properly on anything else. Now God designed the human machine to run on himself. He himself is the fuel our spirits were designed to burn, or the food our spirits were designed to feed on. There is no other. That is why it is just no good asking God to make us happy in our own way without bothering about religion. God cannot give us a happiness and peace apart from himself, because it is not there. There is no such thing.[14]

Real freedom is being able to do what you were made for, a gift found by walking, day by day, with the Creator. To achieve it, a relationship first needs to be established by accepting God's forgiveness through Christ. Once we become sons and daughters of God in this deeper way, God gives us His Spirit. The Spirit gives us power from within to conquer the slavery of sin and to discover the freedom to love.

## Real Freedom is Experiencing God

The God of the Bible is the God of possibilities, of the impossible, of walking on water, of slaying giants. True freedom comes when we experience this great God, when we stand in awe of all that God can do in and through us.

For too many years, we have heard that students identify best with those who are unsure of their faith. No way! Teens need examples of the real thing, of lives free in the wonder and experience of the living God. We, as adult leaders, need to experience God and God's provisions in order to create the thirst of hope in teens. They are inwardly crying out to find God. Douglas Coupland eloquently described that hunger in *Life After God*:

Now – here is my secret; I give it to you with an openness of heart that I doubt I shall ever achieve again, so I pray that you are in a quiet room as you hear these words. My secret is that I need God – that I am sick and can no longer make it alone. I need God to help me give, because I no longer seem to be capable of giving; to help me be kind, as I no longer seem capable of kindness; to help me love, as I seem beyond being able to love.[15]

We are the emancipated slaves who, with wild abandon, show that the chains can be melted away! When on the road, I often share with teens the liberating feeling of serving the awe-inspiring and intimate God of the Bible. The students do not stand back in arm-crossed skepticism; they salivate with hope at the possibility of being loved, of experiencing freedom to do what they were created for. After observing me for a few days to make sure I'm for real, they start to ask questions, and they allow their hope to turn to desire to experience God themselves. They are intrigued at the freedom I have in talking to God, and they look with real longing at the fun I have in doing good.

In movie *The Shawshank Redemption,* opera music permeates the prison yard via the heroic efforts of Tim Robbins' character – a Christ figure. A prisoner, played by Morgan Freeman, later says that of the moment, "for a few moments we felt free." Jesus is like opera music in the prison of everyday existence. A personal relationship with Jesus sets us free – even in adverse circumstances. We must get in touch, via our imaginations, with the transcendent reality of the "Jesus opera," which gives meaning and direction to everyday existence. And we must be the loudspeakers through which that opera is played to the next generation.

## Real Freedom Is Active

Many of North America's early settlers braved dangerous passages in order to have the freedom to worship. They took action so that they could be all they were meant to be. Since then, though, freedom has become something we thought we could pretty much take for granted. We forgot that we still have to work hard to do good. We didn't realize that our wonderful freedom came via action. September 11 eradicated our naïveté. After the tragedy, both youth and adults expressed new levels of compassion. As Christians, we should not have to depend on disaster to motivate us to act. Youth groups should be known for the brave actions we take for the homeless, for flood victims, and for children around the world. It is personal acts of care that unleash personal expressions of freedom.

A young boy came up to me after one of our meetings and asked me to pray for him. His only parent, his mother, had just lost her job. It would take a week or two for social assistance to kick in, and he wasn't sure they had enough food to last. When I went home, my wife and I started to pray for him. We stopped in mid-prayer and looked at each other. Why were we praying about this instead of acting? We went out and bought a backseat's worth of food. We drove to the boy's house in the middle of the night, and attempted to leave the food on the front doorstep without being caught. Cars kept driving by, and we had to hit the dirt several times. Finally the front porch was filled. We left a card on top of it all reading, "From God," rang the doorbell, bolted down the lawn, hopped into the car, and tore out of there laughing. We cranked up the music as we were praising God on the way home. We felt so free, having taken action in God's name!

Every youth worker knows people who could benefit from such generosity. Here are some suggestions: Offer babysitting for single moms, fund a memory-making holiday for a less fortunate family, or take an exchange student along on your group's ski trip.

## Real Freedom Includes Freedom from Legalism

Many teens come to my church from churches of the law. One such teen had parents who did not have a dynamic relationship with God, but did a good job "observing" religious rules. One Sunday evening, his family was travelling on the road. His mother had a urinary tract infection and required a washroom break. But his father refused to stop the car until after midnight. He did not want to make anyone work on the Sabbath through their use of a public washroom. But his wife could not wait that long, and embarrassed herself in front of their children as they drove. Why would God require that of her? No wonder this young man wants nothing to do with a God like that.

In our churches and ministries, we have an opportunity to model the freedom we have in Jesus. But we need to show youth how that is a life free of legalism. (In the theological context, legalism means that rule-keeping is valued above God.) Legalism negates God's grace in our lives. It is not the spirit of how Jesus interpreted Old Testament laws. Jesus was emphatic that healing a man's withered hand on the Sabbath (Luke 6) was more important than the injunction to avoid work on that day. There are too many dream-stealers in our churches, people who cling to the rules and traditions of the past, people unable to see with the eyes of faith and possibility. Many teens see the church as nothing more than a bunch of laws. I have a great friend in my church who, though firmly in middle age, has an enormous impact on our students because of his sense of freedom. When he came to Christ, he was set free from a restrictive denominational structure. Now, if anyone in the youth group asks about rules that are not central to the biblical message, he shouts, "Freedom!" We emphasize not the rules of *don'ts*, but the freedom to *do*, to be all we can be.

Freedom is the message of Galatians: stepping from laws designed to meet God's approval to entering an intimate relationship with God based on the relationship Jesus modelled with his Father. Freedom means living with the same abandonment to God and to others that Jesus had. Churches that do well with teens work hard to discern the spirit of God's desires for our lives without adding a pharisaical length of religious rules. Let us think deeply beyond the rules, to understand the principles behind them.

### Real Freedom Includes Approaching God Imperfectly

We need to teach teens that we can come to God with our imperfections. He would rather we approach Him imperfectly than not approach Him at all. At each of our services, someone walks through the crowd with a microphone to take prayer requests. I love it when the teens pray for each other and experience the freedom of coming to God. I'll never forget one young woman who prayed for the health of her close friend. You could tell she was not a seasoned religious prayer as, with shaky microphone in hand, she said, "Hey, God, this is Jolene. My friend, like, she is really sick, and I guess it may be okay if she died, because she would be with You, but it would, like, really suck for us! God, I know You don't have to, but could You do something about this? Well, I guess that's all I have to talk about right now." The place erupted in applause at the heartfelt words, at the freedom of this young Christian.

To make your church a youth-friendly place of worship, you must allow your kids the freedom to express themselves without worrying about being polished or grammatically correct.

## Model Real Freedom

In *The Book of Learning and Forgetting,* Frank Smith outlines two types of learning. "Official" learning required hard work of the sit-in-your-seat-and-study variety. It relies on reinforcement and tests. Much of what we "learn" in this environment, we forget. Smith encapsulates the alternative, "classic" learning in seven familiar words: "You learn from the company you keep." Classic learning is lifelong and happens almost without our notice. Smith notes that "we learn from the individuals or groups with whom we identify." (He also dryly observes: "I have never heard a parent say, 'I'm not worried about the gang my son goes with – he's a slow learner.'")[16]

Our very lives should whet the appetites of teens for freedom and make them curious about the experience of real freedom. Students need to learn about the freedom in stopping to pray in the middle of McDonald's, the freedom in taking a street person out for something to eat, the freedom in being spontaneous.

The true message of freedom is not taught in Sunday school, but in how you walk through the world. Are you free to forgive, free to enjoy God through worship, free to talk about spiritual things without embarrassment? Are you free from bitterness?

The best youth workers I know have a living relationship with God, and they cannot keep silent about it. With the psalmist, they say, "I will extol the LORD at all times; his praise will always be on my lips. My soul will boast in the LORD; let the afflicted hear and rejoice. Glorify the LORD with me; let us exalt his name together" (Ps. 34:1-3).

## Allow Youth to Invest in the Program

Many churches have adapted the Victorian adage "Children should be seen and not heard" to read "Teens should be seen in our services but definitely not heard!" It is imperative to allow youth significant input into the creation of programs – including the main services. I have seen churches with vibrant youth programs give entire services over to teens, including the teaching, the music, and the prayers. Proud parents and adults show up in droves to support their youth. Other churches give youth positions on boards and make them a part of the decision-making. Some pastors include youth in their sermon preparation, so they can learn the language (including humour!) needed to deliver sermons that connect with the younger generation. Still other churches have youth or adult executives who informally query youth about the direction of programs. Consultation with youth and inclusion of youth is an absolute must in any successful church.

## Allow Free Time

Teens' lives are pressured; they long for free time. The recent raising of educational standards across our country, coupled with extra lessons, has left our teens gasping for free time. Meetings outside of church buildings give a sense of freedom. A Sunday school class at a donut shop will be remembered years from now. Almost every youth event we hold extends into a fast-food restaurant after the official meeting is over. The students and leaders all order a drink or an ice cream and sit and talk, hopping from table to table, laughing until the drinks come out their noses. This is where the best counselling happens. The students have the freedom of time and space to talk to the leaders – and they do. Any work of God that was started in our meeting will likely come up at our unofficial gathering. Leaders pray for such opportunities to listen, to advise, to pray with students.

Every adolescent is involved in trying to break free from the cocoon of childhood. At this crucial time, youth workers must strive to counteract the messages of false freedom and to demonstrate and speak out about the true freedom: "O taste and see that the Lord is good!"

## To Do Today

- When you must write a list of rules for a retreat, make sure to phrase them in a positive way. For example, turn "no boys in girls' rooms" into "boys stay only in boys' rooms."
- Develop a devotional for your group on what true freedom is. What points would you make?
- Start a discussion group about what is good about being an adult. Have some cool adults hidden during the discussion, then have them come out to react to the teens' ideas.
- Run a day camp in which the elderly and teens work side by side to help the children of the area.
- Plan something spontaneous for your next youth meeting. Don't tell the students you are going to do it – let them be refreshed by the surprise. With no announcement, flash up instructions on an overhead (or on PowerPoint). For example, state that the first person to give a shoelace to the speaker will get a prize.
- Start a secret group with your youth. Give it a name like "Angels in Action." Have a night where you go out and give things to people, leaving only a note with the name of your group on it.
- Organize a prayer time in your morning service when prayer requests are taken and (surprise) the teens are the ones who pray for the adults.

- Plan a coming-of-age party for those turning sixteen. (Or fifteen, or seventeen – whatever you think is appropriate.) Give them a list of all the adult privileges they now have in the youth group and in the church.
- Schedule free time at retreats.
- Rent out a local restaurant that does not usually serve breakfast in the morning. Have a morning brainstorming meeting at which all the students have the freedom to dream for the youth group.

# CHAPTER FIVE

# Marinated in Music and Media

A group of teens is preparing for their yearly retreat. Friends have arranged themselves into carloads before any official list could be drawn up. Now there is one smattering of "leftovers" – those teens who do not belong to a particular friendship clan. Their next step is to choose the best vehicle to ride in. Easy. It has nothing to do with the size of the motor or comfort of the seats – it's all about the music. Which car has the best system and the best selection of music?

The other day I overheard three first-year college students talking about how they are just like so-and-so from a television show. They chuckled, talked, and smiled in exaggerated form for the "camera," as they role-played and re-experienced a scene from the show. They saw the program as a very real part of their lives.

If you ever need a good discussion starter, ask teens to name their favourite movies. This simple question will inspire hot debate, laughs, and lots of discussion as each tries to narrow down the expansive field of favourites. Music, movies, and television together create a marinade that permeates every pore of teenagers' beings.

## Survey Says: Music, Television, and Movies Have a Huge Impact on Teens

It would be impossible to list the specific music that teens are listening to these days – by the time this book hits the shelves, many of those bands will be mere memories. Music runs the gamut of human emotions and interests. Some of it brings freedom or comfort or inspiration; some dehumanizes women or advocates a diversity of perversions. We won't take the time to outline areas of rot in the music world. Others are doing an effective job of this already. Our purpose here is to understand teens' fascination with music, and then use that understanding to assist the adults walking with them in their spiritual journey.

Movies and television also have an impact on teens, but the impact appears to be less than that of music – even though teens spend more time on a daily basis watching TV than listening to music.

### TABLE 5.1 **Impact of Music**

- 90% of teens get "a great deal" or "quite a bit" of enjoyment from their music. Only friends rate higher as a source of enjoyment.

- 86% of teens listen to music "daily" while another 13% are listening "weekly" or more. Only watching television rates higher as a source of activity.

- 53% of teens claim to be influenced "a great deal" or "quite a bit" by music.

- 42% of teens jam or work on music "monthly" or more.

- 21% of teens attend music concerts and 18% attend raves "monthly" or more.

- Teens listed rap/hip hop (18%), alternative (15%), and pop (11%) as their favourite types of music.

*Bibby, PTC 2000 data set*

### TABLE 5.2 **Impact of Television and Movies**

- 92% of teens watch TV daily, at an average of 2.7 hours a day.

- 60% of teens claim to get "a great deal" or "quite a bit" of enjoyment from television.

- 60% of teens watch videos at home weekly or more often, and another 33% watch them monthly or more often.

- 40% of teens claim to get "a great deal" or "quite a bit" of enjoyment from watching videos.

- 16% of teens attend movies weekly or more often, and 79% attend them monthly or more often.

*Bibby, PTC 2000 data set*

The time spent in media-related activity rivals the time spent in school, but far outdistances the hours spent in such activities as working at a job, reading a book, or attending religious services.

Relative to their elders, teens have a deep level of trust in the creators of media. In media literacy courses, which are increasingly prevalent in schools these days, every media institution is given a more positive rating by teens than by adults. We should be careful to respect the influence of these forms of communication in the lives of youth.

TABLE 5.3 **Average Annual Hours a Teen Spends in Various Activities**

| Activity | Hours per Year[1] |
|---|:---:|
| Attending school | 1000.0 |
| Watching television | 989.2 |
| Listening to music | 954.9 |
| Working at a job | 339.0 |
| Watching movies at home/theatre | 224.8 |
| Reading | 144.9 |
| Jamming/working on music | 112.8 |
| Attending concerts/raves | 86.4 |
| Attending religious services | 36.6 |

*Bibby, PTC 2000 data set*

TABLE 5.4 **Confidence in Media Institutions Across Generations**
(% indicating "A Great Deal" or "Quite A Bit")

| | Teens | Young Adults | Parents | Grandparents |
|---|:---:|:---:|:---:|:---:|
| Newspapers | 60 | 42 | 37 | 42 |
| Radio | 48 | 41 | 37 | 42 |
| Television | 44 | 28 | 29 | 30 |
| Music industry | 54 | 28 | 25 | 26 |
| Movie industry | 60 | 26 | 22 | 18 |

*Bibby,* Canada's Teens, *2001: 245*

# Why Is This the Case?

Why do media and particularly music rate so high in teens' enjoyment of life? We did not want to make the mistake we adults so often make: forgetting to ask them directly. So we sent out an e-mail to several lists of teens, asking for their opinions. Within minutes, our inbox started to click, click, click with their replies. (Are some of these teens on-line all the time?) Some wrote about movies and television, but music was always pegged as most important to them. Here are some of the replies we received:

> Music is important in my life because I love to be able to express what I'm feeling through music. (Laurie)

I basically listen to music as much as possible and the reason for that is that some of the words really touch me inside or it might refer to what I go through sometimes. I also find that reality of the world is so horrible at times and I block it out for a minute by listening to music. (Kristy)

My specialty is music, while listening to music, I can escape reality. Listen to the tunes, singing alone. All I listen to is basically Christian music, so it describes my love for God. It relates to me, problems in my life, and it says how others feel about the same problems. It's like getting advice, without talking to anyone. It tells you how others deal with certain situations in their lives. It's better than books, cause it's shorter, they both tell stories, but after listening to music, it gives you something to do. You can sit down, pick up a guitar, and play along. It occupies time, gets you out of reality. And since I live in the country without a car, I have a lot of time. Music also has the power to change your mood. Every time I'm feeling down, I put on a set of headphones, they're good cause they block out the outside noise, and turn something awesome on. (Brian)

Wow, music is a huge part of my life. I listen to a variety of music both Christian and Non-Christian. Though sometimes some of the Christian song lyrics written by Matt Redman, Vineyard, Darrell Evans, and etc....may clash with the non-Christian philosophies of life, from artists such as Eminem, Limp Bizkit, Snoop Dogg, and etc (the extra g is not a typo!!!). But I guess speaking from a Christian's point of view, I can honestly say that when I listen to my Christian music I truly do feel the music and mean the words that I sing. When I listen to my non-Christian music it's basically because it sounds good to me, but the lyrics, most of the time, have no real relevance to my life and are listened to for the pure hype of the tunes. Nevertheless, Christian music still Kicks!!! Whooo!!! They have all of what Non-Christian music have, and then some...hehehe. (Hanson)

I think that the number one reason that music is so important in a teens' life is that it's a kind of escape from reality. I know when I am feeling any strong emotion, the very first thing I want to do is find a song that goes along with how I'm feeling, and play it as loud as possible! Often this is a positive thing, but it can be a disaster if you use music to feed emotions of anger or depression. When you are a teen you listen to a lot of music, probably because these are the most stressful years of your life. Blaring music all the time allows you to forget about the thousand and one things you have to do tomorrow, and instead opens up a subconscious world of hopes and dreams and emotions. Like I said, that can be fantastic or terrible. (September)

## Music as Escape

Did you pick up the reasons these teens listen to music? The most obvious one in these and many other replies was that teens use music as an emotional escape. When life seems too overwhelming, music is chosen as an outlet. Such an escape mechanism is especially appealing during the teen years, when an increase in hormones turns up the emotional volume. Mary Pipher, in her excellent book on saving the selves of female adolescents, writes:

> A friend once told me that the best way to understand teenagers was to think of them as constantly on LSD. It was good advice. People on acid are intense, changeable, internal, often cryptic or uncommunicative and, of course, dealing with a different reality. That's all true for adolescent girls.[2]

The emotions of adolescents are raw and displayed much more visibly. Visit any high school after a car accident involving a teen death. You will observe groups huddled and crying in the hallways. Many of these teens may never have met the victim. At the funeral, if there is an open microphone, you will see many teens weeping, standing up to say, "I never knew this person, but...."

Teens' emotions are extreme and changeable. Even small events can trigger enormous reactions. A bad mark on a test creates despair. As Pipher observes, "Girls have tried to kill themselves because they were grounded for a week or didn't get asked to the prom."[3]

Since relationships are so centrally important to this age group, teens agonize over any relational change. Because they are so sensitive, they are also apt to misread the body language of others, and interpret any negativity as directed at them. A bit of gossip, a look of disgust from another, and they are flooded with thoughts of suicide or violence. In the midst of this inner turmoil, music is the drug of choice.

When there is silence around us, we start thinking. Try it yourself: Drive to work tomorrow with no music playing, and notice how many more thoughts go through your head. Teens often want to shut out the hurtful thoughts that plague them. Music is thus the backdrop to after-school life. It is played in shopping malls and in cars, and is turned up even louder at home. When they listen to music, their minds can stop replaying the latest fight with a friend of family member, or the latest poor mark on a test.

## Music as Soundtrack

The more imaginative teens see themselves in a fantasy movie-world, complete with soundtrack. Most of us experience an ongoing internal narrative; we frame our experiences as a story we tell ourselves. As Steven Crites writes, "It seems intuitively clear that we anticipate by framing little stories about how things may fall out. The whole of experience as it is concentrated in a conscious present has a narrative form."[4] Because most teens believe they live life on a stage, under the constant observation of others, they frame their experiences as though they were the plot of a movie.

By adding music to the movie of his life, a teen's internal narrative takes on a whole new dimension. With the soundtrack of the right movie playing, he can walk into a room with the panache of a hero. This idea is perhaps illustrated best in the popular television comedy *Ally McBeal*, in which music is essential to character development. One character, a self-proclaimed "funny little man," uses the music of Barry White to bolster his confidence. While he hears this music in his head, his posture straightens, his chest thrusts forward, and his head is held higher.

## Music as Advice-Giver

Teenagers look outside their homes for clues to identity and values. Musicians represent an alternative set of values and lifestyle choices to draw from. Parents may not understand; friends may not identify with their feelings; but somehow, as they share their emotions through their music, musicians get to the heart of exactly what teens are going through.

This is true not only for reflective music, but also for "hype" music. A drop-in centre worker I know analyzed a song with the kids in his drop-in. Although it told a story of violence, they loved it. They did not understand the story behind the song (even though they could repeat every word); all they heard was the chorus, which hammered home a feeling they felt regularly. The writers of the song captured a teen emotion and used it as bait to hook the kids. Phrases like "It wasn't me," or "I just got to be free," are heart-felt cries that teens connect with. They "get" the raw emotion of the repeated line, along with the emotional climate of the music.

One teen wrote that the advice that seeps through many songs is self-destructive. Some songs advise teens that it is better to cut themselves than someone else when they are dealing with anger. Others suggest that they can only trust themselves.

Teens have to realize that not all musicians are good counsellors. Many musicians are working through their own emotional problems aloud. But teens see them as people who are being real and vulnerable, and they easily identify with these brave "heroes" of honesty.

## Movies and Television Hold Tribes Together

The marinade in movies, videos, and television is far less an internal influence and much more a collective activity. Teens say these media have less personal impact than music. They are, however, instrumental in connecting peer groups. Various students told me that movies were a "social tool"; that television gave them something to talk to their friends about; that visual media helped them "fit in with others." One wrote, "Like most people, there are times that I really have the urge to just go see a really good movie, but most of the time it's to be with friends."

These teens are saying that visual entertainment functions as "social cement." Teens watch television and movies not just for something to do, but also to "stay in the know." Watching every episode of your tribe's favourite television show is a necessity; missing one means you cannot participate in lunchtable conversation. This generation has turned the traditionally isolating experience of watching TV into an experience of community. I know several sets of teens who phone their friends during the commercials of their favourite TV shows to check on their responses. One chagrined father told me he learned his daughter was on the phone for the entire half-hour program so she could talk to her friend about the show as it played out. He was waiting for a phone call and was none too happy.

Friendship tribes know all the cool lines and poses from the latest movie. Hang out in a movie theatre for a while and watch the groups come in. Tribes arrive in animated conversation – already starting to live the movie together. Try to find any teen coming in to watch a movie alone. Or take a minute the next time you're at a video store to observe a group of teens choosing a video. It is a communal activity. Every person in the tribe has a say about which movie to rent.

I performed a wedding recently on a movie theme. The bride's music as she came down the aisle and the design of the dress were from a recent movie. The parents of the couple, scratching their heads, couldn't understand how media, as a communal life event, linked with the wedding – another communal life event.

The experience of visual media can be compared to a ride on a roller coaster: Teens participate not just for the experience itself, but also for the feeling of being strapped in next to a friend. Douglas Rushkoff, an observer of teen culture, calls movie-watching a communal hallucination.[5]

Experience is the name of the game. Surround sound and big-screen televisions crank up the experiential dial. Channel surfing through the legion of channels becomes a living interaction with the media. One teen wrote, "[the experience] can take us to a place so far away from here that when you get brought back down to earth you feel amazed."

## What Does This Mean for Youth Work?

### Respect the Power of Popular Culture

Teens' connection with the visual media runs very deep, and if we wish to build relationships with them we must treat that connection seriously. A young woman I know was deeply affected by a movie in which the main character was a subtly manipulating and domineering person representing death. This woman – who was experiencing tragedy in her life at the time – left the movie thoroughly convinced that this character represented God's action in her life. I assured her that God did not act as she described. I had not seen the movie, but immediately after our conversation I rented it. Only then did I fully understand the connections that this woman was making, and why. I took media's influence on this woman seriously enough to become educated myself, and, as a result, she knew I cared, and took *her* seriously.

### Avoid Seeming Negative

Jesus ate with sinners and hung out with commoners and outcasts. He used imagery from first-century agrarian Palestine – sheep, bread, seed, light, and salt – because he was not suspicious of that culture. He did not tell his audiences to turn to 2 Chronicles, chapter 3, but was passionate about meeting them with good news on their terms.[6]

In Acts 17, St. Paul went to the people he desired to reach – on Athens' Mars Hill. Despite being disturbed by their way of life, he spoke positively of their culture. He quoted the common poets of his day as a springboard to sharing his message of hope in Jesus. "God is not far from you," he said, affirming their search for truth.

We need to have the same attitudes toward youth culture, using it to help us convey our message instead of alienating our youth by only decrying it. Our pop musicians are the poets of today, and Hollywood is a strategic pulpit addressing pressing social issues. We need to let these media touch us, to be aware of what they are communicating, because these are the reference points that will help us reach our mainstream youth.

## Let Youth Teach You

Some youth pastors listen to all the top radio stations to find out what their students are listening to. They spend hours in front of MTV and in movie theatres to see what their students are seeing. The problem with this strategy is that it takes a good deal of time! And the top songs, musicians, and movies change the very next week. I have found it much easier to ask the teens what they are into, and listen and watch some of it with them. What one loses in the illusion of being "hip" and "in the know," one gains in the humility of being taught by the teens – and they love to teach us. Why not sit at their feet and learn? While you do so, ask yourself, "How does this song tap into the emotions of my teens? How does this movie tap into their values?" Then be ready to start conversations surrounding the themes you and the teens see. Learning from your teens gives you a window into their souls.

## Connect Emotionally with Teens Via Active Listening

Emotions are important to teens. We as leaders should be filling the place of musicians and identifying with our teens' feelings. Their friends and family are often either afraid to ask about feelings, or don't know how. Talking about emotions requires what counsellors call active listening. Say a young man tells his adult volunteer he didn't make the basketball team. All too often, the adult will say something like: "That's okay; it's not the end of the world. I think you're pretty good at it anyway." An active listener, on the other hand, would respond with something like: "How are you feeling? I would feel pretty rejected right now." The teen may agree, or may help the volunteer to get the feeling right: "No, I don't feel rejected – I feel embarrassed! All my friends were on the sidelines when the coach read out the cuts for the team."

An active listener interacts, asks, tests out various kinds of feelings until she gets it right. This skill results in a growing attachment to and relationship with a real live adult, who can be closer to the student than any recording artist. An adult volunteer I had just trained in active listening was driving a group of teens back from a retreat, and attempted to start a conversation with the teen sitting in the passenger seat. His questions brought out only one-word answers, until the volunteer remembered what I had taught him and simply asked about the teen's feelings. As he related to me afterwards, the conversation shot off, and the teen spent the remainder of the trip confiding in him.

## Use Music in Your Ministry

Use music as students arrive at youth events, as people walk out on stage during a youth service, when you are driving with the teens – it is an essential backdrop whenever you want energy. We usually have music playing for our student games night – at which we reach out to community teens – but about once a year it breaks down in some way. The youth night is music-less. The students walk in with weird looks on their faces. They realize something is wrong, but they can't quite put their fingers on what. Those who don't eventually notice that the music is gone simply complain that the night "sucked."

## Use Youth Praise Services Strategically

Because of the importance of music in teens' lives, youth praise services (services in which youth from various religious groups and denominations gather to sing songs of worship to God) appeal to them. In my area, new youth praise services spring up every two months or so, in smaller and smaller communities. I recently spoke at youth praise service of 200 high-school students, in a town whose population was only a thousand. Many universities hold praise services right in their campus pubs. McMaster University in Hamilton, Ontario, was the first to start this trend, with a program called "Church at the John." They now boast 600 students, some of whom will stand through the two-hour service at a campus pub named The Downstairs John. From coast to coast, other campuses host praise services with such names as Church on Tap, Church in the Box, Church in the Hangar, and Church in the Turret.

In another community, a youth service shut down a year ago. I talked to the leaders and students to find out why. The hour-long service had had a half-hour message. More and more announcements came from all kinds of groups in the area. They had to leave time for a drama. Near the death of the event, the actual music content had been whittled down to four songs. Take a wild guess why the service didn't live.

In my youth service, we guard the worship time. We don't allow people to bring in announcements or give long appeals. If someone has an area event, we ask them to hand out flyers at the door as people leave. And we make sure that the worship music is played at the best level of quality we can muster. After listening at home and in their cars to stereos and CDs with near-perfect sound, there is only so much poorly played music teens will tolerate.

Teens come to services looking forward to singing their favourite worship songs in a familiar way. (They are all traditionalists at heart.) That is why we don't bring in different bands to play at every service. When songs are played in different styles, the students' worship is distracted. They wonder why the visiting group "isn't as good." The songs at a worship service must be known, so the students can break free from singing to connecting with God through the song. We have found that a song needs to be performed at least three times before people have a real comfort level with it. So we introduce only one or two new songs at each worship service. If we try to squeeze in more than that, the students have to concentrate on too many new tunes and words. Their worship experience is taken away, and they stop coming.

## Think Through the Debate over Christian vs. Secular Music

Some say that, since teens listen to secular music anyway, we should use it in youth work and teach teens to listen to it with their minds as well as their emotions. Many in this camp also believe that secular music is better-quality music. Others say we should encourage students to listen only to Christian music, which gives teens a godly friend who "enters their bedrooms" with advice. Besides, the people in this camp counter, there is quality Christian music in virtually every music style that youth listen to.

To us, the issue is not nearly so black-and-white. Both secular and Christian music celebrate wholesome life experiences and prophetically address society's most crucial issues. The theology and lifestyles of both secular and Christian musicians can, at times, be suspect. And the quality of both types of music runs the gamut from truly magnificent to downright mediocre. We need to be wise and prayerful about all music intake. We must move beyond the naive view that "Christian" equals good and "secular" equals bad. All types of music and media require discernment.

Music is an important source of enjoyment for teens, and it is crucial that we not make abstinence from their particular type of music a condition of acceptance. If we make turning from the secular a law, we can fall into a very destructive legalism. Yet if we do not recognize the pull of the "friends" who talk through the music, we are refusing to admit to the emotional power of music. We need to listen to secular music with the teens we care about. As we listen with them, we can ask them questions not only about the specific piece of music and its lyrics, but also about why they are drawn to that style of music.

On the other hand, it is during the teen years that many people become Christian. Teens often find that some secular lyrics create thoughts that inhibit spiritual growth. Many teens go through a period when they want their minds and spirits cleansed of the influence of other world views. They decide to turn from secular music to listening to music that leads to pure and positive thinking, so that they can dive deeper into God.

Every youth group is different. In ours, we sometimes analyze secular songs during devotionals. But the music we play (and we always play music) is Christian contemporary or worship music. The students get used to it, and even start to play it themselves at home and in their cars. Where else will they come in contact with quality Christian music if not in youth groups?

## Use Visual Media

As we have discussed, teens see music as a conductor for their emotions. But they see visual media as stories to be communally experienced. References to movies or television shows can be powerful tools because, when we use them in our talks, we can evoke a whole storyline with a few simple words. Movie clips can be easily used to illustrate points. Within seconds, teens' hearts and minds connect to the subject at hand – and it remains a communal experience. If I want them to think about the power of evil, I play a short clip of Darth Vader saying, "Luke, if you only knew the power of the dark side." The students laugh with recognition, as whole movie scripts go through their minds about the pull of things that are dark. We take movie clips and add our own voice-overs to introduce our discussion topics. For example, we have Tom Hanks confessing that he is gossiping to his volleyball in *Castaway*. The teens are much more open to being confronted with their weaknesses through media. We all laugh at the familiar as portrayed on the television screen.

Because the visual media create such an ideal forum for communal experience and discussion, they are often used by youth groups to explore issues and experiences. I know of a youth group that designs its youth night around a popular television show. Instead of trying to compete with the show for the attention of the kids, this youth pastor recognizes its draw, and turns on the television for the youth group. They watch the half-hour show together, then discuss the subject matter when the show is over. In this way, he avoids the risk that the kids will just stay home to watch the show and miss out on the group experience. At the same time he validates the importance of the show to their lives, and uses it to teach them.

Many television shows are ideal for provoking discussion on serious issues and life values. Right after September 11, for example, *The West Wing* quickly produced and aired an episode in which the White House underwent a lockdown because of a terrorist threat. Much of the show attempted to bring meaning to recent events with insights such as "The Taliban is to Islam what the KKK are to Christianity." The writers and producers of these shows tackle these issues from their particular world views, which you may or may not agree with. Why not tackle the issues and the world views head-on? As you watch your favourite show, keep a tape running. You don't need to show the students the whole episode. Serious issues are often dealt with in a few minutes and can launch a debate, a lesson, or simply a discussion of values.

Keep in mind, though, that pop culture tends to glorify revenge. The cutting put-downs of sitcoms, the portrayal of women as objects, the subtle preaching that bad is good and good is bad are all funneled into our homes via the television screen. We need to ask ourselves what we are allowing ourselves to be entertained by, and have the courage to talk to our teens about it.

In an age when only 10% of teens crack open a Bible in a week, the church still takes Scripture seriously, not just for doctrine but for living. So use movies as a way back to the Scriptures. Believe it or not, videos often portray the gospel. The gospel is "in the air"! It's everywhere – in songs, in images, in expressions. Point out the places you see Scripture. "Did you know that that expression comes from Isaiah?" "Do you know that Molson beer's slogan 'I AM' is a term for God from the book of Exodus?" "Do you know that Jesus told that Good Samaritan story first?" God doesn't leave himself without a voice. Help youth hear it.

## Encourage Teens to Participate

Teens today want to participate. We can no longer simply try to entertain them. At many of the events I speak at, a band will come in to play. I have seen the stand-and-deliver kind of band, where there is no participation, clear an auditorium. The musical tastes of teens are so fragmented that only the very few who may know the band will stay and be "entertained." Yet I saw a single guitar player hold a crowd of a thousand by involving the students in the music. She got them to sing certain parts with her or clap at different times, and she interacted with them by relating stories. The crowd had a role to play, and stayed to participate.

Singing, clapping, moshing, body-surfing, dancing, lifting hands – however it's done, worship must be participatory.

We cannot ignore the reality of the media marinade our teens soak in. We can dream of days gone by, but God has planted us here in this time and age. We must have the courage to evaluate the music/media mix and redeem those pieces for the Kingdom that we can.

## To Do Today

- Next time a teenager tells you a fact, try asking how he or she feels about it.
- Organize a monthly movie night, at which you watch the latest video release and then discuss it. (Preview the movie and be ready for fast-forwards where needed.)
- Watch a television show, or part of one, during your youth group time and use it as a launching pad to discuss issues that are brought up in the show.
- Develop a media team to give advice on what movie clips to use during your messages or talks. (This means that you need to complete your messages before the day of the event.)
- Create a suggestion box for songs that students would like to discuss.
- Schedule a training night where you train your adult volunteers in active listening.
- Make sure you have music at every event. Put a rotating group of teens in charge of organizing the music, so your group can experience a diversity of musical styles.
- Visit a praise service in your area. Ask area youth pastors where to find one, and encourage the youth you know to make it a regular event.

# CHAPTER SIX
# Digital Divides

An enthusiastic young man approached me in a local bookstore. I had befriended him at the community college where he was a student, but we had not seen each other for months. He had first come to me in a state of depression, his career and relationships unravelling. In time, we had become friends. But when school ended, we drifted apart. Now he wanted to catch up. When we met for coffee, I was amazed at the change in his disposition. He appeared confident, took initiative in conversation, and shared upcoming goals. What had turned this young man around? A girlfriend? A church young-adult group? Wisdom learned from our sessions? No – a computer video cam! He shared the story of mounting a digital cam on his computer, starting his own chat room, and of all things, "body building for the camera." Now he interacted with a community of people from around the globe. His site got thousands of hits per month. His insecurity and loneliness had disappeared. "If so many people want to interact with me over the Net," he reasoned, "there's no way I'm the loser people in the past thought I was!" It was most impressive that a virtual community could be so meaningful to his sense of identity.

I often run into stories like this one, in which new technologies enhance the lives of youth and young adults. A handful of couples in our churches met over the Internet and are now happily married. A college girl I know prefers to develop virtual relationships with guys because that way "they don't get physical." One youth worker witnesses to her faith via chat rooms; another overcame dyslexia thanks to a read-and-write software program, and now maintains relationships with his youth via e-mail. Many teenagers carry on five to eight conversations at the same time on messenger networks like MSN.

We live in an accelerated age of computer and media technology. We've heard it all before: In the last forty years, we've moved from mainframes to personal computers; from journals to Day Timers to PDAs; from LPs to CDs to MP3s; from 8mm film to VCRs to DVDs. Even as I write, more regions around the world are being added to our high-speed, networked global community. And there is no sign of an information slowdown.

In such an age, we need to address some obvious questions: How are youth engaging with new technologies? Does the computer "hype" match the reality, or do we need to identify emerging myths and misconceptions? Given the anecdotal success stories we hear, do digital communications technologies offer opportunities for youth ministry? How should we think about the interface between technology and youth ministry?

## Survey Says: Teens Aren't Quite as Enamoured of Technology as We Think

Many social analysts have dubbed the millennials the digital generation. Some refer to them as screenagers.[1] Others speak of children, empowered by new technologies, taking the reins from their boomer parents and making inroads into all areas of society.[2] These descriptors are true, perhaps – but only for very small minorities of youth. Let's go to the survey data for a reality check.

### The Myth of the Computer-Savvy Teen Generation

Despite the ubiquitous presence of computers in schools, only 42% of teens say they use them daily, a figure lower than that for most adult generations (see Table 6.2). And while more teens than adults report having home computers, on average, teens use them less than adults. There is one exception: E-mail, which appeared on the public scene in the mid-nineties, is used more by youth and young adults than by boomers and boomer parents. Still, young adults communicate by e-mail more than teens do.

Digging deeper, we learned that 80% of teens use a computer every week. In addition, 69% of males and 54% of females access Web sites weekly or more often, while 56% of males and 60% of females will communicate by e-mail in a seven-day period. Monthly figures for teens jump to approximately 90% for computer use, 80% for Web site access, and 70% for e-mail.

These data suggest that, while the vast majority of youth have both skill and accessibility to digital technology, computers simply enhance their lives rather than define them. Many teens use computers to download a favourite song, check their Hotmail account, play a computer game in their spare time, put a query through a search engine, or browse a new Web site, but that's the extent of it. Many teens who talk daily on

MSN are simply using the computer as another telephone. Sure, certain teens are very "wired." Some maintain their own Web sites. Others frequent on-line fantasy games, participate regularly in chat rooms, or spend outrageous amounts of time on sports and music sites. A few maintain deep relationships with friends in locations around the globe. But only a small segment of the youth population (perhaps 5-10%) spends enough time in front of the screen to fit the "screenager" stereotype (see Table 6.1). On the other end of the spectrum, 15% of teens have no access to a computer at home.

### TABLE 6.1 **Computer Use Distribution by Gender**

(Refers to the 86% who have computers at home)

| Daily # of Hours | % of Males | % of Females |
|---|---|---|
| 0-1 | 12 | 17 |
| 1 | 35 | 43 |
| 2 | 22 | 21 |
| 3 | 12 | 7 |
| 4 | 7 | 3 |
| 5-6 | 7 | 3 |
| 7+ | 5 | 6 |

*Bibby, PTC 2000 data set*

In another survey question, teens were given an opportunity to list their favourite Web sites. Only 44% of teens liked a site so much they felt inclined to name it. When I go on-line to check out sites my teens have recommended, even very popular sites such as Phatphish.com have only ten to twenty others visiting at a time. Despite the popular stereotype, computers do not dictate the lives of most teens.

## Males vs. Females

There is some evidence that males and females experience computers differently. For example, males use computers slightly more than females.

Males are also more likely to report a higher level of enjoyment from their computers (56% vs. 39% of females) and from the Internet (48% vs. 37%). In addition, males far outdistance females in video game or computer game use: Incredibly, seven in ten young males play digital games weekly or more often, while only three in ten female teens do.

Females, however, use e-mail more, by a 38% to 28% margin. Many female teens communicate regularly by e-mail with both local and geographically distant friends.

It appears that, while both genders use computers for information and education, females are more likely to use them for relational purposes and males for recreation or entertainment.

## Young vs. Old

Much has been made of the fact that the younger generation is the first to be able to access information without the guidance of authority figures. Most teens say, "Big whoopie deal!" to this. My hunch is that, given the major transitions they are negotiating, youth receive precious little consolation from being part of this favoured generation. From their perspective, it is not a big deal if you know how to download MP3 files, run a scanner, or add macro-media to a Web page – even though these are things their grandparents can't necessarily do. Rather, in an age where there is an overabundance of data bytes, youth want someone to assist them in turning information into wisdom. What is useful? What works for others? What is the best of the good out there? Teens have a deep craving for spiritual direction and mentoring relationships in this technological era.

TABLE 6.2 **Computer Use By Generation**

(% indicating "Yes")

|  | Teens | Young Adults | Parents | Grandparents |
|---|---|---|---|---|
| Have a computer at home | 85 | 80 | 75 | 50 |
| Use a computer daily | 41 | 59 | 51 | 29 |
| Use e-mail weekly | 58 | 68 | 53 | 31 |
| Average daily time spent on a computer: | 2.1 hours | | All Adults: 1.4 hours | |

*Bibby,* Canada's Teens, *2001: 237*

These data suggest that computer savvy-ness happens later in the life cycle, and is perhaps linked to factors such as adult employment.

A related stereotype says that change is the only constant for the younger generation; thus they roll with it much better than do older generations. The data, however, don't support this notion. In the teen survey, respondents were asked to agree or disagree with the statement "Canada's uncertain future makes it hard to plan for the future." Fifty-seven per cent of teens agreed. This was higher than every adult cohort (53% of grandparents, 46.5% of young adults, and 41.5% of adults agreed). In addition, both adults and teens were given the opportunity to state how much they were bothered by "so many things changing." Thirty-eight per cent of teens were bothered "a great deal" or "quite a bit" by this concern. No other generation of adults rated as high.

Clearly, the stereotype misses the mark. Rather than being comfortable with change, large percentages of youth find the degree of social and technological change that they are forced to negotiate disturbing. Adults have been forced to adapt to change enough times that they have learned the necessary coping skills.

What are the implications of this for ministry? I have intentionally surrounded myself with academic, financial, ministry, and spiritual mentors of an older generation. They have been a huge gift to me. I have made it a strategic focus to pass their insights on to the younger generation. My Day Timer has regular meetings with older mentors slotted in, and my college office has a cappuccino maker, an easy chair, and a steady stream of youth and young adults who come by for spiritual direction. I have not run into a single youth or young adult, no matter how "hard" he might initially appear, who does not crave input from wise adults.

## The Impact of Computers and Television vs. Human Relationships

On average teens spend 2.1 hours a day using computers and 2.7 hours watching TV. When asked how much enjoyment they get from computer use, and how much it influences them, teens rated computers much lower than television – and even lower than face-to-face interaction with humans. While 60% of teens claim to get a "great deal" or "quite a bit" of enjoyment from television, computers (47%), the Internet (42%), and e-mail (33%) ranked considerably lower. At the same time, 29% of teens saw television as a major influence in their lives, while only 11% gave the same rating to the Internet.

Teens rated virtually every human relationship – mother (81%), friends (78%), father (70%), another respected adult (58%), and teachers (36%) – as more influential than technology. In high-tech times, people continue to desire high touch. We must never forget that quality relationships, not technology, are at the heart of youth ministry.

# Why Is This the Case?

Our capitalist world thrives under the illusion that an endless array of new technological products is desirable. "Upgrade, so you won't fall behind," advertisers say. The seductive hype is designed to bring all who are "hip" – or at least want to be – onto the wired bandwagon. The frenzy has been profitable for companies with products to sell and the growing numbers of people (especially those in power) with stocks to maintain. Just think how many times in the last ten years you have had to upgrade your own computer. Even now, it is becoming obsolete, as larger memory banks with faster speeds and smaller components are created.

The very few teenagers who have sold their Web sites for millions get much more than their share of media play. They have proved a useful carrot to attract teens looking for a lucrative future. But at present, computers are simply one more information-carrying system – and to their minds computers have always been around. (My tweenager is shocked when I tell her that I didn't have a computer when I was a teen.) Teens recognize that computers have relational, informational, and recreational value – but most prefer the non-virtual options.

Before we can talk about the use of technology in youth ministry, three myths need to be dismantled.

## Myth #1: Computers Are a Great Place to Build Community

In my neighbourhood, the coffee shop is the favoured hangout place for many people, both young and old – including me. It is a constant bustle of activity, as people meet up with their friends and interact. There is a joyful energy to the place. Just down the street is an Internet café. It is rarely full, but even when it is, there is a dull functionality to the interactions between people. I'm not convinced that the relationships being formed on-line can compare to the deep connections being made in the coffee shop down the street.

While some teens, such as my video-cam body-building friend, find unique value in technological ventures, the majority do not find the Internet a great place to make intimate connections. They miss real physical intimacy and sensory stimulation. Teens are now holding LAN parties: They put their desktop computers into one room and hook them up together, so they can still see each other and hear the cries of dismay when they "kill" their friends in cyberspace.

"Much of what happens over the networks is a metaphor – we chat without speaking, smile without grinning, and hug without touching," states Clifford Stoll, author of the thought-provoking book *Silicon Snake Oil: Second Thoughts on the Information Highway.* "On my screen, I see several icons – a mailbox, a theatre, a newspaper. These represent incoming messages, an entertainment video, and a news wire. But they're not the real thing. The mailbox doesn't clunk, the movie theatre doesn't serve popcorn, and the newspaper doesn't come with a cup of coffee at the corner café."[3]

A guiding principle for church Internet use is that it cannot and should not replace a formal church assembly. According to Ken Knight, communications director of the Presbyterian Church of Canada, "The Internet is a communications tool to be used by the church to improve efficiency. Elements such as fellowship, touch and tears can be experienced only in face-to-face meetings. And these elements are essential to 'being church.'"[4]

A friend of ours recently completed a doctoral thesis that asked churched youth who spent time on-line where they experienced community. He compared bonds made via church, religious youth groups, and the Internet. Youth groups came in a resounding first place and the church came in second. The Internet was rated lowest by almost all the youth as a forum for establishing connections, because two things essential for community – trust and authenticity – were extremely difficult to establish without ongoing face-to-face interactions.[5]

Trust and authenticity are indeed huge issues for millennials, as they are for youth workers. I know a young youth worker who is being courted by a church in another region of the country. They have e-mailed, shared resumé and church profile information, and spoken by conference call. But when the church board invited the youth worker for a formal candidating weekend, she said to me, "No, I'm not ready for that. First I need to fly out and have time to hang out to get a sense of whether this relationship could work." She needed to build trust face to face before she could consider a greater commitment.

Teens have on-line aliases – they create different ages, sexes, and places of origin for themselves. Our church intern from Australia, Racheal Humble, lives and ministers on-line. She notes, "Internet ministry is a double-edged sword. You can really get the gospel into people's hearts because they're more open to hearing and engaging at a deeper level because of the 'anonymity' you can get on-line. That same anonymity, however, means you've got no way of making sure that people aren't pulling the wool over your eyes. It's pretty edgy stuff. You get vulnerable and share your passion for Jesus with someone, never really knowing if they're mocking you the whole time, or if He's using you to change a life for eternity."

## Myth #2: Teens Value Gimmicks over Content

Youth chuckle at what some religious groups put onto Web sites – and on television, for that matter: everything from a winking Jesus to "Turn or Burn" invitations. In my experience, gimmicks do not entice young people. A youth I met accessed a Web site on which the hand of God flashed lightning onto a screen, and an image of Jesus appeared, along with the words "You touch Jesus and he'll touch you." He confided in me that if his friends saw the site they would not be impressed: "You win people with content. Cheesy gimmicks only hurt your message."

A digitally savvy youth worker friend of mine agreed. He gave me a quick tour of the evolution of the Web. Originally, Web sites were mainly texts. Content was important during this phase. Then images were added, basically cut-and-paste clipart. Now we have entered a third phase, in which video imaging, background music, and colour coordination are common. The creation of Web sites is now best left to those with professional design capabilities; it is beyond the skill level of most Net users. Content remains important, but content is now more than just text. It is visual, audible, and interactive. Quality is paramount. As one young commenter stated, "If it doesn't move, it isn't a Web site."[6] My youth worker friend goes even further: "If it doesn't move you, it is not a Web site I'd frequent." Many youth would agree.

Youth do use on-line daily devotional sites that have easy-to-get-to, quick, inspirational content. A friend of mine works with a whole office of young twenty-somethings. Their job requires them to sit in their cubicles in front of their screens and punch numbers. Many happen to be Christians, and the first thing they do when they start work is log onto their favourite devotional site to receive a personal thought for the day.

## Myth #3: Computers Promote Solitude

"People who enjoy computers don't enjoy spending time with others."

"If teens spend too much time looking at a computer screen, their brains turn to mush, and they lose their ability to interact directly with people."

The survey data generally do not support these statements. Bibby's analysis of the survey data found that computer activities, if anything, related positively to higher levels of relational enjoyment.[7]

This "socially deprived" critique is often levelled at junior- and senior-high students who are home schooled via "cyber high." My nephew and three nieces have been schooled this way. They are four of the most socially adjusted teens I know. The crucial factor in their success is not the amount of educational time spent at the computer, but their holistic and joyful approach to life, mixed with large doses of quality social interaction with compassionate and consistent adults and teen friends.

# What Does This Mean for Youth Work?

## Recognize That Technology Is a Tool

Technology has no magic characteristics. It is not an end in itself, but a means. At times, it can increase the exposure of a great message. Think, for example, how many around the world have been inspired the widely popular Introduction to Christianity Alpha video series.[8] Technology can also assist by making data storage and retrieval easy and efficient. I've been amazed by how fast I can get information – like last night's Stanley Cup highlights – via the Web.

Technology can help people maintain close communication despite geographical distance. We, as authors, are able to write a book together even though we live in different parts of the country. I love how my cell phone keeps me in touch with my soulmate whenever I'm out of the house. But in most instances the relationship is already there; technology simply makes it easier and enhances it.

The Internet is a tool: not the Antichrist, and not the Saviour.

Some ministry is initiated via cyberspace. A friend of mine has witnessed to her faith many times in chat rooms, and even showed someone on-line how to begin a personal relationship with Jesus. I am sure that many of us know of such examples. But most people need connection to a body of believers that models face-to-face trust and authenticity to advance in their spiritual walk. Many years ago, I took a communications course that aimed to spread the great news of Jesus' love through Christian radio. The researchers found that communication that was not face to face could help people in the initial "fact-finding" stages of a spiritual journey. However, when commitment was needed or a new value needed to be grasped, the vast majority of people required direct involvement with a person and a group.

## Use Technology to Enhance Relationships, Not Replace Them

One frequently raised concern about new technologies is the degree to which they fragment populations. We are haunted by the spectre of a world chained to computer screens. When I think of my friend body-building for his virtual cheerleaders, I wonder whether he will learn a downside to his ongoing exposure. Will these friendships prove satisfyingly intimate in the long run? I have heard my share of heartbreaking stories of failed attempts to turn e-mail friendships into face-to-face ones. Some virtual relationships work; many do not.

Still, I see a real need to affirm the value of connections maintained via the Web. I have chatted with youth pastors who speak of how e-mail creates a forum where they can maintain a deep level of interaction with certain youth. Many youth pastors keep their relational channels open with live MSN conversations as they work on their computers. Virtual relationships can delve into intimate terrain more quickly and deeply than face-to-face dialogue. But the bond developed in this way does not necessarily sustain the relationship when personal interaction is introduced into the equation. This reality must be respected and wrestled with.

Because of the prime value of relationships at the core of the universe, technology ought to lead toward rather than away from improved face-to-face interactions. On this principle, I celebrate the present value of my body-building friend's Web cam. Through his relational success on-line, he has improved his relational abilities in real life. However, I value the use of voice mail, for example, only where it increases the sanity of busy people who go on to translate their stored energies into quality relationships. The goal is always be to increase quality human interaction and joyful personal contacts.

## Develop a Web Site for Your Church Group

When setting up a Web site, the key is to include ways for people to create human interaction from virtual interaction. The church's address, youth group phone number, and e-mail addresses for youth coordinators should be readily available. In the words of Quinten Schultze, architect of a course at Regent College called Faith and Cyberspace, the purpose of virtual communication should be to enhance oral communication.[9]

As you create your site, ask yourself, "What do we need this site for?" The purpose of the site will dictate what it should look like. If it is an arm into the broader community, then it needs to have aspects that draw the seeker in. One church in our area posts a funny cartoon of their pastor. Their home page holds a large sign that reads "God Hates Religion." A site like that certainly has appeal for the average person; they will visit on the advice of a friend, just to see the cartoon. But if the site does not then connect them to a person, outreach is hindered. Sites that focus on outreach need to provide direct connections to someone willing to answer spiritual questions, perhaps in a chat room.

If a site's purpose is mainly to advertise youth events, times, and places, it will look quite different. The information should be no more than two clicks away. And remember: People grow impatient if offered more than seven choices on any one page. (Researchers have found seven items to be the maximum amount of information the average human brain can handle. When given any more than that, people lose concentration.)

Another purpose for your site may be to build the image of your youth group. One group I know posts pictures from their last event. Friends invite friends to see pictures of themselves. These youth start to think: "Hey, this youth group is cool. It looks like they had a great time last week. I need to make sure I am there next time." This site makes a strong connection by advertising itself as a group of friends.

All sites should dispense information that is up-to-date and pertinent to the group. Over time, the hits to your site will decrease unless current information is continually posted. This is a long-term commitment that must be assessed at startup. In our church, we have assigned several youth to the task of making sure our Web site is not the same each week. One teen keeps the e-mails updated, every week adding a handful of new e-mails and changing or removing a handful of old ones.

In our highly digitalized world, people have come to love the freedom afforded by technology. It's great to be able to browse a Web site and anonymously access information on an organization. Since this freedom actually enhances communication over the long term, browsing should be encouraged on our sites. But we need to include open, non-threatening routes to deeper human and divine relationships.

Web site technology for some youth may play the role that icebreaker games played for an earlier generation. Youth can check out a group on-line. (If the site is set up for them to do this anonymously, it needs to clearly explain the order of service and other pertinent information.) Incoming youth will be served if the Web site clearly indicates what can be expected if they make an appearance. They can check out the sights and sounds of the service at home and break down some of the barriers that "church" may have for them.

My church has cards available for people to hand out to friends and invite them to our services. The cards have information about our church and cool graphics – and the Web site address is prominently displayed. Teens find out through our Web site that we aren't as boring as they imagined, and then feel more willing to make face-to-face contact.

In my church we hold a massive youth service every second and fourth Sunday evening. We use e-mail to remind teens – who often forget what day of the week it is, let alone what week in the month it is – that the service is in two days. And we set up a chat room, which is now used regularly by the small handful who are "into that kind of stuff."

E-mails are not only awesome as reminders, but are great for prompting feedback. One section of our Web site allows students to rate our last youth service via an e-mail link or message board. And it's not just feedback we get, but creative ideas for the future! We offer prizes for any crazy ideas that are shot our way via the Web site and are used at a service. Our dream team, which comes up with creative things to do in our services, reviews the submissions. If an idea is a winner, we award a prize to the teen at the service, thus providing a connection from cyberspace to reality.

E-mails are fast, which gives rise to two ministry possibilities. First, a person can send out fifty individual and personal e-mail encouragements in a half-hour – even without mass e-mailing. Try it some night and see what happens. Second, the convenience of e-mail means no one gets regular mail anymore, so the relational value of a handwritten note is boosted. I see many handwritten notes adorning the walls and tabletops of the young people I minister with.

Digital cameras are fabulous. I know of one church that sent a digital camera along on the youth group mission trip, and then posted daily reports on the Web. That next Sunday, the entire church watched clips of the kids in action half a world away – before they returned home. Bonding, informed prayer, and shared memories were created via technology in an unprecedented way.

In the enthusiasm to begin Web site ministries, we must remember that they appeal only to a small fragment of the youth population. It is a fragment that we are called to reach, but we should never fool ourselves that through Web youth ministry we are performing our full duty to youth. Sites with millions of hits do not translate into millions of people influenced. I myself am likely the source of a hundred hits to my own church's Web site. For a variety of reasons, many youth are disconnected. We cannot afford to let computers become another "us vs. them" division.

## Respect Generational Differences

The digitally savvy teenager stereotype is reinforced for me every time my butt is kicked soundly by my son at X-Box games. When I then see some young youth worker negotiating his PDA with an ease I only dream of, I sink lower into my own techno-insecurities. It is at times like this that I am in danger of forgetting to keep the main thing in youth ministry – relationships – the main thing.

The world of rapidly changing technological options presents increasing challenges for those of us who are older. When younger youth workers speak with glowing admiration about their downloadable PDAs or DVD-integrated PowerPoint presentations, I celebrate the enhancement that technology gives to their lives and maintain an open mind about what I might learn from them. At the same time, while I cannot imagine life without e-mail, I don't impose my fervour for it on my parents' generation. They have managed to live without it up till now. The telephone works as well for them as e-mail works for me. I trust my Palm Pilot–toting co-workers will maintain the same mercy towards me.

## Remember Technology's Drawbacks

Technology is frustratingly unpredictable. Most of us have experienced how it can complicate tasks and relationships. An e-mail from a friend illustrates this point: "My youngest brother and I spent an evening trying to make computer games work on our home network, so that my younger sisters would be able to join us in playing them. Eventually, after nearly five hours of fiddling, uninstalling, and reinstalling, we were able to get a really old game working on our top-of-the-line machines. It's silly, really. Our machines are three times faster than required to run these two games that we used to play on our 486s."

In my friend's case, networking computers together and playing an old game was leisurely and bonding. But others who experience technological complications feel frustration and, eventually, anger. For them, technology becomes a barrier to relationships rather than an enhancement. Their time would be better spent in uninterrupted, focused interaction with others than in wrestling with a tool that's not working.

The proper use of technology such as e-mail and cell phones requires learning and following new rules of etiquette. It is still courtesy to not answer the phone when in the middle of a face-to-face conversation. Increasingly, we need to remind our students to turn off their cell phones and pagers during services. I spoke in an upscale part of Toronto last year to over a thousand students and fought throughout the service with the buzz of cell phones. Christian youth workers need to take these issues seriously in both their modelling and teaching.

As well, the Internet raises an array of ethical, moral, and criminal issues that range from basic concerns about loss of privacy and access to previously illegal material to downloading and dissemination of other people's property, to exploitative scams and downright theft.[10] It is hard to imagine an Internet user who has not been affected in some way by the spread of Internet porn through spam e-mails or links from other sites. Most youth workers I have spoken to have experienced it at least once, and our youth are in the same boat. This material, which treats women as objects, is seeping into the male mind. We youth workers need to address this issue with candour and frankness.

The new medium of communication is changing our world just as much as the telegraph, the telephone, and television changed the world for previous generations. In the face of this change, we must remember that we are still humans made in the image of God, with an internal need to connect. Our relationships with each other remain of paramount importance. We should embrace the relationship-enhancing power of the new technologies, but we must use them with care.

## To Do Today

- Give a few teens the reins to develop your group's Web site.
- Create business cards with your youth group's logo and your Web site in prominent positions. Print "Check us out!" on them. Give them to your students to give to their friends.
- Send out e-mail reminders of when your youth meeting is.
- Set up a computer in the corner of your youth room where students can type in their e-mail addresses for your address book.
- Hold a Web night, at which students show the group their favourite sites. Make sure you are ready yourself with some cool Christian sites.
- Have a digital camera ready at the beginning of your youth outreach. At end of the evening, show the students pictures of themselves coming in.
- Conduct a discussion with the males of your group on how to stay pure while surfing the Net.

# CHAPTER SEVEN

# Dancing with Consumerism

**M**y family and I were on a vacation to beat all vacations. We were camping, so we had with us all the stuff that comes with camping. We had food, tents, sleeping bags, sand pails, chairs, and our canoe. Our car was so loaded down, the tires almost rubbed against the wheel wells. Our sleeping bags hung out of the canoe, which was strapped to the roof. Chairs were bungee-corded to the top of the trunk. Semi-inflated beach toys pressed against the windows of the back seat. The front seat held three of us, with our bodies half hanging out of the windows. We couldn't help but notice the smirks of people who drove past us. On our way to the campgrounds, we decided to visit the grave of my wife's mother, since we were in the area. For one crazy moment as we pulled into the cemetery, everyone around turned to look at us. I felt compelled to shout out the window to the gawkers, "Yes, we *are* trying to take it with us!"

If ever there was an image that could depict the millennial generation, it might just be this: a vehicle loaded with the accumulated stuff of years of consumption. While earlier generations have been economically disenfranchised, this generation has optimism and vision to earn and consume. And they do it with a passion. Romance is overrated, school may be boring, but consumption is a dance worth dancing.

## Survey Says: Teens Are Buying More than Ever

A large part of a North American teen's identity is tied up in leisure activities that place them in the clutches of advertisers. On average, youth spend almost three hours per day watching television, and another two hours on the computer. Advertising is sometimes the highlight of sports events. Sports stars are paid more for product endorsement than for their athletic prowess, and music stars sponsor soft drinks. As one marketing executive wrote, "We consider a music video to be a long-format commercial."[1] Table 7.1 lists a smattering of entertainment options and the degree to which teens embrace them.

TABLE 7.1 **Common Teen Activities**

(% of teens who participate)

| | Daily | Daily to Weekly | Weekly to Monthly |
|---|---|---|---|
| Watching television | 95 | – | – |
| Listening to music | 86 | 98 | 99 |
| Using a computer | 41 | 80 | 91 |
| Doing something to stay in shape | 31 | 81 | 93 |
| Accessing Web sites | 25 | 61 | 78 |
| Following sports | 21 | 52 | 69 |
| Keeping up with the news | 17 | 66 | 82 |
| Playing video/computer games | 12 | 47 | 67 |
| Using a cell phone | 13 | 40 | 56 |
| Watching videos at home | 8 | 60 | 93 |
| Attending a sporting event | 3 | 15 | 42 |
| Going to a movie | 1 | 16 | 79 |
| Going to a music concert | 1 | 3 | 21 |
| Going to a rave | 1 | 6 | 16 |

*Bibby, PTC 2000 data set*

## Teen Spending

A study pegged the annual number of trips to a shopping mall by the average teen at fifty-four.[2] For many a teen, a mall is a place to belong, to hang out with friends, to reinvent oneself. Clothing tops the list of items purchased. A new wardrobe can turn heads at school, and can do wonders to change one's demeanor. As Anne Sutherland and Beth Thompson put it, "The growth in tween and teen clothing business has been the talk of the retail industry for the last few years. Some sources claim that apparel is the fastest-growing kid market."[3] The average teenage girl has seven pairs of jeans, and the average male, five pairs.[4]

When they're not hanging out at the mall, teens can often be found at the movie theatre. Kids and young adults aged twelve to twenty make up 16% of the U.S. population, but they buy 26% of the movie tickets.[5]

To take advantage of this fact, massive entertainment and theatre complexes have sprung up across North America. Now when teens go to see a movie, they can also get a full meal, visit a candy store, and play video games or mini-golf, all without leaving the theatre. In the process, a lot of money changes hands.

Youth are also making their presence felt in the burgeoning on-line purchasing market. In the spring of 2000, a Canadian survey found that 55% of teens were "window-shopping" on-line, and 10% went on to make a purchase. The 45% who looked and didn't buy were stopped from purchasing only by the need to have a credit card.[6] (This problem is being quickly resolved by credit-card companies, which have created cards with a limit that is prepaid by parents.)

American girls alone are estimated to spend $60 billion annually on consumer items.[7] The 3.3 million teenagers in Canada have $19 billion a year burning holes in their back pockets. That's about $107 per week, per teen, in disposable income.[8]

## Preoccupation with Money

With all this consumption, one would think that the pursuit of money would be a preoccupation for teens. And for many it is. According to the survey data, about 50% of teens, both male and female, hold down jobs during the school year. Of those employed, 40% work less than ten hours a week, 54% work eleven to thirty hours a week, and 6% report working more than thirty hours a week. Assuming a wage of $7 per hour, teens that have a job earn, on average, about $100 a week. Many also get an allowance (an average of $20 a week) and other cash gifts from Mom and Dad.

Approximately 14% of teens have cash squabbles with their folks "very often," while another 25% have them "fairly often." But roughly 60% of males and 63% of females claim they seldom or never disagree with their parents about money. That may be because this generation of parents is accustomed to indulging adolescents. As one CEO who taps the teen market states, "[Today's youth] have access to incredible amounts of capital. Typically, daddy's little girl gets what she wants and moms don't have to be dragged to the mall."[9]

Despite employment and parental largesse, more than 50% of youth worry "quite a bit" (or more) about not having enough money. Only 16% of teens state that they are seldom or never bothered by this issue, and for some the anxiety is acute: 24% of males and 23% of females are bothered "a great deal." A recent drama performed at a local high school carried this concern as a subplot. The play, called *Juvie,* shared the stories of a diverse range of teenage girls in a juvenile detention centre. One girl spoke of the shame and anxiety of being so poor she couldn't afford designer clothing. Taunted constantly by her peers, who called her a loser because of her shabby appearance, she resorted to shoplifting clothing in an attempt to gain acceptance – and ended up in juvie.

TABLE 7.2 **Teen Financial Concerns (Three Snapshots over Time)**

|  | 2000 | 1992 | 1984 |
| --- | --- | --- | --- |
| % of teens bothered "a great deal" or "quite a bit" about lack of money | 53% | 71% | 54% |
| % of teens who think the economy is a "very serious" or "fairly serious" problem today | 25% | 57% | 37% |

*Bibby,* Canada's Teens, *2001: 180-181*

Yet a look into the recent past uncovers a surprise: Youth today are less concerned about their personal finances than their counterparts of 1992 were. It appears that teens' personal-finance concerns parallel what happens in the economy. When the economy is good, teens' concern is relatively low. When the economy falters, financial anxiety increases.[10] Today's teens were brought up at a time when North America's economy was booming. A recent print ad illustrates the point: A contented tot lies sleeping. "Why is this child smiling?" asks the caption. The emphatic response: "Because he has lived his whole life in the biggest bull market in history."[11]

In many ways, this is the story of today's youth. Conspicuous consumption comes naturally to them. Like the baby boomers, they have been raised in good economic times. MTV's senior vice president of research says, "Times were kind of tough for the teens who grew up in the early 1990s. Now kids rule. No parent wants to be accused of not spending time with their kids or giving them anything they want. The economy's really great. In many ways, things are amazing for them."[12]

As of 2000, teens felt pretty good about their economic future: 96% anticipated owning their own home; 85% thought they'd get the job they wanted when they graduated; only 44% expected they'd have to work overtime to get ahead; 79% expected to be more financially comfortable than their parents; 61% planned on sticking with the same career for life; and 49% felt that the national debt would be paid off within their lifetime. Furthermore, money figured prominently in career considerations; 96% of teens stated that being paid well was a very important or somewhat important feature in the choice of a job.

Teens' optimism gives us pause. Those who are brought up in good times have the kernel of hope that previous generations did not. Still, we wonder if youth have developed the inner fortitude needed to navigate serious economic and social downturns, should they come.

# Why Is This the Case?

To understand teen consumption patterns, we need to understand the broader economic and social environment in which teens live. We know that teens consume, but we need to look closer at who is producing. Enter youth's dancing partner: the corporate marketers.

These partners are eager, flexible, sophisticated companies that are often part of the network of a multinational conglomerate. The world is becoming increasingly democratic and capitalistic, and, with the rise of free-trade agreements, goods and services flow easily across borders. Capitalism is efficient: Global conglomerates find ways to manufacture more and more goods at cheaper and cheaper rates. As a result, they have a lot to peddle. And recognizing an opportunity for profit, they have taken direct aim at the youth demographic. A browse through the advertisements in any teen magazine highlights the diversity available to our youth.

## Companies' Role

During the recession of the early 1990s, economic analysts noticed that, while adult-oriented products, such as soap and sewing machines, were struggling, sneakers and soft drinks were holding their own.[13] At the same time, the number of teenagers was starting to grow for the first time in years as the children of baby boomers came of age. Moreover, a whole new trend was developing: Teens were becoming more technologically savvy than their parents and were advising their parents on the purchase of many household items.

The entire economy made a concerted effort to become hip for the youth demographic. Research companies targeting the teen market began to spring up. Many hired youth focus groups or young adult researchers to sniff out the next cool trend. *National Geographic* reported that some companies were even hiring young people – called "cool hunters" – to travel the world and report trends that could be translated into mass-marketed products.[14]

The companies that succeeded the best at targeting the youth market adopted a new strategy of selling "brands" rather than products. Naomi Klein, in *No Logo,* explains the strategy: "The product always takes a back seat to the real product, the brand, and the selling of the brand acquired an extra component that can only be described as spiritual. Advertising is about hawking product. Branding, in its truest and most advanced incarnations, is about corporate transcendence."[15]

Take a look at the T-shirts teens wear. Fewer and fewer have sayings on them, and more merely have brand names. The primary function of brand, Klein argues, is to market a lifestyle, an idea, a value. Nike's CEO, Phil Knight, announced in the late '80s that Nike is "a sports company" – its mission is not to sell shoes, but to "enhance people's lives through sports and fitness" and to keep "the magic of sports alive." Other corporations are following suit. Polaroid is not a camera; it's a social lubricant. IBM doesn't sell computers; it sells business solutions.

To turn brands into philosophies, complete with desired attitudes and behaviours, companies put massive amounts of energy – and money – into marketing. Marketing budgets have soared. Nike's advertising budget, for example, went from $50 million to $500 million between 1987 and 1997.[17] At the same time, many companies have begun to outsource the production of goods (along with the hassles of factory upkeep and worker care) to contractors. The genius of this strategy is that companies can focus entirely on marketing, while improving their bottom line by outsourcing manufacture to the lowest bidder. (These are often found in Third-World sweatshops, where labour costs are low and tax breaks are plenty.)

Another advertising strategy encourages "relationships" with products, since relationships with people are so complicated. "What do you mean guys aren't into commitment? He's had the same backpack for years," says one ad.[17] A *TV Guide* back cover featured a handwritten note that said, "Dear John, We've had so much fun together. But sometimes things happen and people grow apart. I don't know how else to say this but I think we should take a break. While I know this might hurt now, I really hope that we can be good friends. Fondly, Nancy." A small caption, complete with logo, at the bottom of the page read: "Thank goodness for Kleenex. If only relationships were as dependable as Kleenex facial tissues." Marketers know the genius of this strategy: As we know from previous chapters, relationships are of paramount importance to teenagers.

Via mergers, the same multi-national corporations that sell products also increasingly control the communication lines that transmit their messages. And they establish contracts with teen icons, especially athletes and entertainers, to endorse their products.[18] Britney Spears and Pepsi struck a multimillion-dollar advertising agreement for global sponsorship on February 6, 2001. This deal was win-win for all concerned. Britney wins: Not only does she get massive amounts of cash, Pepsi ads and a sponsored tour keep her in the limelight. Pepsi wins: Britney's endorsement will influence her worldwide following of young soda drinkers. Stockholders win: PepsiCo stock rose following the announcement. And the American dream stays alive in the younger generation: One of their own has struck it rich. Teenagers are winners, because they are fans of a winner. This, indeed, is "the joy of Pepsi."[19] These deals, however, only last till a "hotter" star comes along. Beyoncé replaced Britney as Pepsi queen for 2003; she, too, will be replaced as her lustre fades.

Companies are working to win over the loyalties of smaller and smaller tribes of youth. Specialized advertisements appear wherever these niche groups congregate and in the media that cater to them. Nike won over skateboarders with the slogan "What if we treated all athletes the way we treat skateboarders?" Skateboarders believe that Nike knows them and has the guts to defend their sport. Who cares whether that's true, as long as skateboarders believe it is true? Products can even be produced with a subgroup in mind, if it's deemed profitable. One catalogue company noticed that 30% of teen girls are overweight; they now see a market for "intimate fashion for overweight kids."[20]

Right now, a hot growing market is children ages nine to twelve. Teen culture began its boom when society recognized a time in between childhood and adulthood. Now society has created the tweenager: those between childhood and the teen years.

Indeed kids are bombarded with a fervid and intentional marketing effort from the moment they are born. As Mike Searles, president of Kids "R" Us says, "If you own this child at an early age, you can own the kid for years to come."[21] Companies believe that, if early relationships with brands can be established, lifelong allegiance is possible.

## Teens' Role

The other partner in the consumerism dance is, of course, our teenagers. As teens search for an identity, eagerly pursuing the "Who am I?" question, they find a quick and easy way to establish identity in the purchase of products. Yesterday I was just a boring person; today I dyed my hair pink, and I now wear all black. I am declaring to the world that I am a different person.

A key advertising approach is to find authentic inner-city youth subculture, package its attitude, and sell it as rebellion to youth in the suburbs. Another is to prey on the insecurities of youth by giving teens an exaggerated notion of what it means to be "masculine" or "feminine." In teen magazines like *YM, Cosmogirl,* and *Seventeen,* advertising, photo spreads, and articles converge to form an image of the ideal woman. As one college student wrote, reflecting on her high-school experience, "I have come to the conclusion that teen magazines are analogous to secular Bibles. They describe a way of life, and outline how teens should live out this way of life. They describe an ideal and list expectations through which teens can try to achieve this ideal." The message young girls are given is: "In order to be happy you will need a boyfriend, and to get a boyfriend you will need to improve your looks." Magazines then offer products, complete with attitudinal and behavioural scripts a girl must follow, to achieve ideal womanhood as portrayed by the ads.

Youth tribes dictate outward identity, indicating the proper gear to wear in order to belong. Advertisers in turn reinforce the distinct tribes that have become commonplace in the landscape of adolescence. Make no mistake: the gear one wears, or decorates one's locker with, transcends style and takes on a spiritual meaning. Like a pen used by Thomas Jefferson, or a violin by Heifetz, the object itself has no greater inherent value, but the value of its meaning may be huge. Students searching for a voice look at the totemic value of items. The type of skateboard, the stickers used on it, the colour of the shirt, the design of the MP3 player all give the person value by the mere ownership.

Although their tribes set the themes of what they want to wear, teens still want to be unique. Observe the tribe of Goths standing on the corner. They all look the same, simply dressed in black, right? But take another look, and you will see the many different ways black can be incorporated into a wardrobe. Teens develop creative uniqueness within the tribal setting. They are drawn to second-hand shops, where they can buy such items as a Peewee Herman T-shirt no one else will have.

Most teens are quite contented. Ninety-two per cent claim to be "very happy" or "pretty happy." Many are realizing a key youth value – comfort: 96% of males and 98% of females claim a comfortable life is "very important" or "somewhat important" to them, and more than 70% of these teens feel they are achieving comfort.

Teens say they are wary of the influence of major corporations, although they continue to buy the products. Only 50% of males and 47% of females have "a great deal" or "quite a bit" of confidence in the leaders of major businesses, and 13% of teens have little or no confidence in them. This suggests that teens are wary when new products are pitched to them. The source of this anti-corporate discontent is probably multi-faceted, with social justice issues, environmental concerns, and a desire not to be bombarded playing key roles.

Still, the majority of teens can't see the relationship between their own comfort on the micro level and the global system that supports their consumption on the macro level. Only 29% of males and 21% of females felt that people in power had "a great deal" or "quite a bit" of influence on them. The rest seem oblivious to the fact that their consumption is directly linked to their status as citizens of one of the world's wealthiest economies.

## Consumerism Hurts

Youth culture is suffering in our present advertising milieu, and four groups are especially vulnerable.

The first group is the economically poor, who are often invisible in a system such as ours. Advertisers make their pitches to those who can afford the products. The media bombard us with stories about the lives of the rich and famous, but we seldom hear the stories of the poor and destitute. But poor people listen to the narratives and the ads, and these unleash longings that cannot easily be met. Many disadvantaged youth fantasize about being rich and carry a sense of frustration about their poverty.

The second group hurt by advertising is youth who do not fit the marketing stereotypes of masculinity and femininity. Many are left disillusioned and discouraged when they cannot achieve the ideals. Fifty-one per cent of females and 38% of males are bothered "a great deal" or "quite a bit" about their looks. A young adult, reflecting on the role that teen magazines had in her teen years, writes:

> I can remember memorizing every page of each issue of each teen magazine, hardly being able to wait for the newest copy to get the stand. I would compare myself to these gorgeous girls and wonder why I could not achieve their beauty even though I did everything the magazines told me. Not only did I faithfully follow all the beauty tips and clothing techniques, but I reli-

giously read every article about "how to get a guy" or "easy steps for achieving love." Yet, I never found myself more popular, beautiful, or with a boyfriend as the magazine promised. During all this time of trying to measure up to the "magazine perfect teenage girl," all I ever found was unhappiness with myself. I believe that I am not a minority and most of the female youth culture is affected by these magazines in a negative manner.

Third is youth who are spiritually committed. More than two centuries ago, John Wesley wrote that over-consumption was a "cancer eating away at our spiritual vitals."[22] What would he say today? Consumerism has become the religion of our time. Advertising co-opts sacred symbols and language to evoke an immediate response. Neil Postman refers to this as "cultural rape that leaves us deprived of our most meaningful images."[23] Eternity is a Calvin Klein perfume, Infiniti is a car, Jesus is a brand of jeans, and "see the light" is an ad for wool. One car is "born again" and another "energizes your soul." An ad for kosher hot dogs pictures the Bible next to a hot dog, with the caption "If you like the book, you'll love the hot dog." "I AM" is a beer ad.[24] Teens who value faith can't help but feel violated when that faith is used in such a trivial manner. But an even more serious problem is that many of them don't even know a violence has occurred. In this milieu, those we reach out to with the good news of Jesus hear our messages as another advertising pitch, and too often miss the awesome value of Jesus for themselves.

The fourth group particularly affected is Third-World youth. Advertising fragments traditional cultures by unleashing desires that were never there before. A few years ago I heard Gwynnc Dyer share a story of a Bedouin village in Egypt that got a satellite dish. Within a few years they had a difficulty they had never had before – their teenage girls were running away to Cairo. Why? They were in search of Nike runners. As marketers target the global youth demographic, they are promoting a uniformity that fragments traditional cultures.

In addition, much of the stuff that is "cool" is created in squalid factories in export production zones by Third-World teens. Naomi Klein tells of taking a T-shirt she had picked up from a Florida Wal-Mart back to the factory in Haiti where it was made. As she converted the $10.87 the shirt cost into the local currency, the girls who made them shrieked in disbelief. $10.87 was one week's wages. In a week they sewed 500 shirts. If we care about the world of people made in God's image, we need to care about this abuse. As some forecasters have said, "Our 'growth-mania' must stop or it will destroy us."[25]

Consumerism hurts all youth by promoting a self-absorbed ideology of happiness that shifts the balance of influence away from community values and people who truly care for youth. Noted media researcher George Gerbner states:

> For the first time in human history, most of the stories about people, life and values are told not by parents, schools, churches, or others in the community who have something to tell, but by a group of distant conglomerates that have something to sell.[26]

What a crime, when parents, schools, and churches have such good stories to tell!

It is from God and other people – not products – that we get zest and vitality, empowerment, clearer knowledge of self and others, and desire for more connection through intimacy. Advertising trivializes and negates the personal connectedness teens really want. One ad I saw recently stated, "Some people need only one man. Or one woman. Or one watch. OK, we can't be monogamous; at least we can be faithful to our watches." We learn from this type of ad that it is far safer to make a commitment to a product than to a person. Ad after ad portrays relationships as dull and ordinary. Individually, these ads are silly, but cumulatively they create a climate of cynicism and alienation that is poisonous to healthy interpersonal relationships. They instill a longing for a product, rather than for a more authentic connection with the people in our life.

In a culture that surrounds them with images of lust and romance, and very few models of long-term love, most teens are growing up totally unprepared for the hard work, give-and-take, and forgiveness needed to make commitments work.

## What Does This Mean for Youth Work?

Happiness and meaning in life cannot be found in an object. Relationships are what lead to fulfillment, and we, as youth workers, must be advocates for good, growing, committed relationships. Youth groups need to teach relational survival skills such as forgiveness and communication. It is no wonder students treat each other as objects when they have so few models that demonstrate how to treat people as spiritual beings. Adults in relationships need to be vulnerable about their journeys. The days of hiding relational struggles are past. These students need examples of real people forgiving each other, sitting down and really communicating, achieving a balance of truth and grace.

As Catholic youth ministry consultant Tom Beaudoin says,

> Taking radically seriously the mystery of God present in all of life has perhaps never been more difficult than it is today, because mystery, unlike almost every other aspect of our identity, cannot be purchased, styled, accessorized, or exchanged. Only God has the copyright and the trademark on the mystery of all human life.[27]

This is the time for students to come face to face with the ultimate relationship, the only one that can consistently fulfill: a relationship with God. Every attempt to fill the internal void is ultimately an attempt to fill a God-shaped vacuum.

The gospel is filled with very personal images of being regenerated (John 3:3 and 1 Peter 1:23, for example) and being given the Holy Spirit. The Bible is filled with an intimacy of walking with God. God came to us in the flesh to show us that He is among us. God made the move to be up-close and personal with us. If we don't introduce our teens to a God who wants to walk with them through life, then we will leave them to continuously search for a fulfillment they will never find.

## Develop Contentment

What does the counterculture of Christ say to the consumerism addiction?

Jesus' solution to those who were building bigger barns to store more assets was to let them know it all goes back in the box.[28] When I was in college, I loved the game Risk. The first time I played it, I quickly understood that world domination was the only goal – nice guys finished last. After hours of playing the game, I won. I looked down at the map of the world, and saw that I ruled the entire planet. It was some horribly early hour in the morning, and my friends all said, "Let's put the game away." I didn't want it to go back in the box. I wanted to savour the win. This is a common feeling, and I'm sure most people would understand it. But God says that at the end of this life all the homes, cars, and toys go back in the box; Only the faith, hope, and love given us through God remain on into the next life – the rest was all part of a big game.

We need to learn the secret of contentment, and develop it in ourselves and in our teens. I believe contentment is achieved by finding your place of spiritual service. Once you have found your true calling and have tasted the joys of working within it, the toys of this world pale in comparison. The open-handed stance of freedom from allowing possession to possess you speaks loud and clear to those caught up in a world of who can grab first. We can model this freedom by giving to others outrageously, letting "our" gifts and possession be used for the Kingdom without regret. I once served with a pastor who was very passionate about freedom from ownership. Every time he and his family moved, they gave away or sold everything but a small handful of mementos, and started over again.

## Provide Jobs Within a Christian Environment

In many ways, teens see jobs as a rite of adult initiation. Yet the majority of workplaces, while teaching some discipline, also teach many other ruthless values. We need to use wisdom when deciding how early our teens can start earning money to buy the things they want.

I would recommend to any and all parents that their teens work at Christian summer camps. The discipline of hard work is found there, but within a tribe that espouses Christian values. The talk around the campfire is on actions and attitudes of eternal worth, not on who has the newest toy. The church can also provide jobs for teenagers, paying them just as much money as any other part-time job, and much, much more in the achievement of things of eternal worth.

Teens are the cheap hands behind so many products. Somehow the values of work need to be separated from the draw of consumerism. Unfortunately, most adults are also infected with the same disease.

## Uphold Delayed Gratification

Addressing a high-school assembly, Rev. Dale Lang noted, "Teens live in an instant gratification era. This has raised their level of expectation. And when they don't get what they want now, they can feel an intense level of anger and anxiety."[29]

Teenagers are increasingly fed the notion that they can have their fun now and pay for it later. The debt-load of the teenagers we come across is staggering. Newly acquired credit cards are maxed out early. I have many young-adult friends who feel compelled to work insane hours while going to school in order to pay off credit-card debts.

In the tribe set apart, Jesus understands money as a way to give to others. He urges us to make a deposit into heaven by giving to those who will never be able to repay us. He teaches us that the seductive lure, the love of money, is the root of all evil.

As youth workers, we must teach a kind of giving that actually costs the giver, that does more than just put dents in surpluses in the bank accounts of suburban youth and adults. For example, youth groups could sponsor a child from a Third-World country; hold a fundraiser to raise money for charities; or volunteer at a local food bank, soup kitchen, or homeless shelter.

## Deplore Idolatry and Envy

We must also discuss the subject of idols. We laugh that people thousands of years ago made things with their hands and then worshipped them. But it's not so different today. Explore with your teens the possibility that they may be giving more "worth" to their cars or stereo systems than they do to God.

I read a book of stories written by teens, and was surprised by the number of tales of envy. One teen bought a set of clothes that another could not afford. One teen's parents gave him a car, while another could not afford one until high school and college were behind him. Envy breaks up relationships, and creates bitter, cynical teens whose focus is on consuming and not on relationships that last.

## Offer Space

We need social places that are not owned by corporations. Quiet places. Places for daydreaming. Places that offer another message, a message spoken consistently, quietly, confidently, so that youth can warm to its appeal: "Beyond the homogenous theme parks of commerce, we may rediscover free spaces in which it is possible to live not only as consumers, but as people who think, and breathe, and love." Youth groups can be great at communicating this message!

We must slow life down. The message in our groups must be that, no matter who you are and where you've been, the party mat is out for you. You count, just as you are, whatever you wear. Your presence is valuable. You belong, and can come and go as you please. We need to take seriously the words in the book of James:

> If a man enters your church wearing an expensive suit, and a
> street person wearing rags comes in right after him, and you say
> to the man in the suit, "Sit here, sir; this is the best seat in the

house!" and either ignore the street person or say, "Better sit here in the back row," haven't you segregated God's children and proved that you are judges who can't be trusted? Listen dear friends. Isn't it clear by now that God operates quite differently? He chose the world's down and out as the kingdom's first citizens, with full rights and privileges. The kingdom is promised to anyone who loves God...God talk without God acts is outrageous nonsense. (James 2:1-6, *The Message Bible*)

Once we have created such a place, it will be so attractive that it will always have a bustle of activity. Connections will become second nature. We cannot change the world of advertising overnight, but we can slowly, one teen at a time, one group at a time, plant a mustard seed of difference and then watch it grow. It works. I know this from experience. Love is the ultimate addiction, and it cannot help but spread outward, like ripples in a pond, if we stay the course.

We also need to provide space for the tweenagers. Although this term is a cultural creation, our nine- to twelve-year-olds perceive it as a real life stage. Junior-high ministry has never been more important. With society setting these kids apart and giving them a unique identity, the church cannot and must not forget them.

## Support "Youth Recycling" Projects

Teens addicted to consumerism can benefit from "youth recycling" projects – environments such as youth drop-in centres, youth addiction programs, and other youth groups that cater to youth at risk. Yes, some groups thrive by keeping their youth pure, encouraging an environment of service to others, and creatively loving and knowing God. But know what you are doing – your group may not be open or appealing to youth who have deep addictions to those aspects of pop culture you have eliminated. If your youth group isn't a "recycling depot," caring for the most broken of youth, do you at least generously support other ministries that are?

## Honour People of All Body Shapes and Sizes

Advertising creates pressure to sculpt the perfect body to fill those perfect styles, and that pressure often results in eating disorders. For years, bulimia – binge eating and purging – has been mainly a female dilemma, but now young males are also getting caught in this horrible trap. Bulimia continues until the body's electrolytes are thrown off and the bulimic person is walking around in a near-coma. People with anorexia perceive themselves as fat no matter what the scales may say. As they deprive themselves of food, their weight drops lower and lower, until their bodies cannot handle even the act of eating. Anorexia is potentially fatal.

Teenagers are especially vulnerable to these diseases, which are brought on by self-loathing. I have often brought in trained counsellors to speak on bulimia and anorexia. Every time, I am surprised when one of my teens has an extended talk with the counsellor afterwards.

We must teach our teens to love and accept their bodies by modelling love and acceptance of ourselves and others, regardless of appearance. Ideally, our group of adult volunteers would have representatives of several different body types and sizes, to help us in this task.

Why do we run after "stuff" so much? We will not be able to take it with us. If our tribe apart honours giving as much as getting, we will all be richer.

## To Do Today

- Plan a series of lessons on each of these subjects: contentment, envy, and delayed gratification.
- Create a monthly activity in which your youth will perform random acts of kindness using their own money and resources.
- Encourage students to make identity collages on their Bible covers, giving them unique totemic value.
- Reassess your junior-high group. If you don't have a group for tweenagers, make it a priority to begin one.
- Start discussions by having each teen describe why an item they are wearing is important to them. In describing a piece of clothing or jewellery, one often reveals something about oneself.
- Start a savings fund for some project, to teach your teens the discipline of time.
- Bring in a psychologist to speak about anorexia and bulimia.
- Assign an adult to raise $20 a week. Use this money to pay a teen for doing work for the church. (We do this – people are more than willing to give, and the teen loves it!)
- Make a collage of pictures of things people idolize. Place the collage next to a poster of an idol.

# CHAPTER EIGHT

# Mind Grinders

Not too many years ago, Western missionaries travelled to foreign cultures and took with them the living faith of Jesus Christ. Along with their faith, they took Western architecture, Western songs, and Western dress. I still have a musty picture in my mind of the brightly shining smiles of African children, all dressed in white shirts and polyester pants, standing in front of their cinderblock church clutching hymnals filled with songs that were written in Europe. Like burrs from a field, Western culture stuck to these foreign cultures and was planted alongside the message of God. We even taught theology from a Western mindset. We tried to prove to animists – who saw spirits in every rock and tree – that there was a spiritual world. How ridiculous! We somehow forgot to address the needs and questions of the specific culture.

As mentioned earlier, North American youth culture is in some ways as distinct as foreign culture, and deserves the same consideration. It is important to know what is on the minds of youth. What questions do teens wrestle with day after day? If we, as youth leaders, can get a grasp of the questions that grind through the minds of youth, then we have a better idea of what to address. Our job becomes clear. If we try to guess what problems are on teens' minds, our ministry attempts miss the mark.

## Survey Says: Concerns Grind Away in the Mind of Teens

### Social Concerns

The data suggest that teen anxieties ebb and flow like the tides of the sea. Some concerns are linked to broad social conditions as teens come of age. For example, nuclear war dominated youth's thoughts in 1984, the economy bothered teens in 1992, and violence in school plagued teen consciousness in 2000 (see Table 8.1). In addition, note that in 1992 teen anxiety overall was higher than in either 1984 or 2000. Reporting on the PTC 1992 data in their book *Teen Trends*, Reginald Bibby and Donald Posterski had a heading "Young People See Problems Everywhere."[1] My hunch is that, for Canadian teens, the harsh recession and restructuring of the early 1990s, the political uncertainty at the tail end of Canada's Mulroney years, and national unity issues linked to Aboriginal communities and Quebec separatism made youth more pessimistic about many other personal issues.

TABLE 8.1 **Teen Social Concern Shifts Over Time**

(% viewing as "Very Serious")

|  | 2000 | 1992 | 1984 |
| --- | --- | --- | --- |
| Child abuse | 56 | 64 | 50 |
| AIDS | 55 | 77 | — |
| Violence in school | 50 | 36 | — |
| Teen suicide | 49 | 59 | 41 |
| Drugs | 48 | 64 | 46 |
| Environment | 42 | 69 | — |
| Poverty | 41 | — | 33 |
| Crime | 40 | — | 48 |
| The economy | 25 | 57 | 37 |
| Threat of nuclear war | 24 | — | 48 |
| Lack of Canadian unity | 21 | 39 | 13 |

*Bibby,* Canada's Teens, *2001: 181*

Most of the things that concerned teens in the early '90s are of less concern to teens today. It appears that, overall, today's youth are less stressed. They have grown up in prosperous times and seem to have a more optimistic base of experience from which to navigate life. But the minds of these teens are still grinding on issues they deem important.

## Child Abuse and AIDS

The number-one and number-two social concerns on the minds of youth today are child abuse and AIDS. Both are global plagues that receive ongoing national and international media attention. Today's youth are aware of Third-World sweatshops where teenagers slave long hours to produce consumer goods for the West. They have heard reports of child prostitution and pornography rings at home and abroad. Headlines have featured child victims of war in Africa, Afghanistan, and the Middle East. Bizarre stories closer to home report kids being caged or physically beaten. And teens have heard that AIDS epidemics reduce life expectancy by half in some African countries. For some youth, the issues of child abuse and AIDS are heightened by personal experience. Emotional and physical abuse are part of the home reality for some. Others fear that, through their own sexual activity, AIDS could one day become a very personal tragedy.

## Violence in School

The area of mental grinding that has risen most since the last survey is concern for safety while at school. In 1992 only 39% of students thought that violence in schools was very serious. That number now has jumped to 50% (59% for females). It is easy to see why. The news media flood our radios and televisions with reports of violence in schools. Parents are driving their kids to school more than ever. Home schooling is skyrocketing, because parents are willing to pay the price of personal time and energy to ensure the physical and emotional safety of their children. Students crave safe places.

## Personal Concerns

Social issues are not the only source of anxiety. Personal concerns also eat away at our teenagers. Table 8.2 identifies the degree to which common problems bother our youth.

### School and Future Pressures

A key mind grinder for students is worry over school and the future. "How do I deal with the pressure at school?" "What do I do when I finish school?" These questions topped the list of personal concerns. School is a central arena in the world of the adolescent, and the future looms large. I run into many youth who are anxious about their personal futures. Parents and teachers are impressing on them that further education is needed to keep their career options open. They feel pressure to maintain A's so they can into the best programs. As one youth stated, "You feel like a failure if you get a B in science."

## TABLE 8.2 Teen Personal Concerns Nationally and by Gender

(% indicating bothered "A Great Deal" or "Quite A Bit")

| | Nationally | Male | Female |
|---|---|---|---|
| Pressure to do well at school | 67 | 64 | 69 |
| What to do when finished school | 66 | 63 | 70 |
| Never seem to have enough time | 57 | 52 | 61 |
| Lack of money | 53 | 52 | 54 |
| Not being understood by parents | 45 | 41 | 48 |
| Boredom | 42 | 44 | 41 |
| My looks | 45 | 38 | 51 |
| Losing friends | 47 | 39 | 53 |
| Wondering about the purpose of life | 43 | 38 | 46 |
| Feeling not as good as others | 36 | 27 | 43 |
| My weight | 34 | 21 | 45 |
| So many things changing | 38 | 35 | 40 |
| Not having a boyfriend/girlfriend | 34 | 36 | 32 |
| Loneliness | 30 | 26 | 33 |
| Depression | 29 | 25 | 33 |
| Parents' marriage | 27 | 24 | 29 |
| Sex | 26 | 30 | 22 |
| My height | 20 | 19 | 21 |

*Bibby,* Canada's Teens, *2001: 36*

## Time

"Never seem to have enough time" ranks number three on the list of personal concerns, with 57% feeling stressed about lack of time. Females (61%) feel this more than males (52%). I can hear you say, "Just wait until they become adults and they will understand how tight time really is!" Well, that's just it. In the race to become adults, teens are feeling the "many-ness" and "much-ness" of life. Journalist Patricia Hersch went back to school for three years to live the life of an adolescent again. She describes her experience: "I was assaulted by a wall of sound activity. It was madness: kids whizzing past me, teachers helplessly trying to slow them down, noisy caverns between the lockers bellowing with voices."[2] In addition to their school responsibilities, teens often have jobs, are involved in sports or other extracurricular activities, and have family and church obligations. The perception of not having enough time can squeeze the joy out of life.

### Money

Another mind grinder for teens is money. They just never seem to have enough of it – 53% of teens considered lack of money very important. Remember that the students polled are not starving. Even though most teens have high levels of disposable cash, many are not content. Credit cards are now being introduced to this age group. Marketing campaigns pummel teens until many believe that their happiness depends on having more stuff – and, therefore, more money.

## Ultimate Questions

As illustrated by Table 8.3, a number of ultimate questions churn in the back of teens' minds. And if tragedy strikes, as it sometime does, these questions flood to the surface.

TABLE 8.3 **The Extent to Which Teens Raise Ultimate Questions**

(% who have wondered)

|  | Often/ Sometimes | No Longer Have | Never |
|---|---|---|---|
| What happens after death? | 78 | 15 | 7 |
| How can I experience happiness? | 73 | 17 | 10 |
| Why is there suffering in the world? | 72 | 18 | 10 |
| What is the purpose of life? | 72 | 17 | 11 |
| How did the world come into being? | 63 | 24 | 13 |
| Is there a God or supreme being? | 56 | 25 | 19 |

*Bibby, PTC 2000 data set*

### Death, Suffering, Happiness, and the Purpose of Life

Seventy-plus per cent of teens wrestle with the issues of death, suffering, purpose, and happiness. It may seem strange that those who are so far from death wonder what lies on the other side. Still, death is perhaps the most frequent private worry of the younger generation. Perhaps Littleton, Colorado, Taber, Alberta, and New York City have much to do with the anxiety. School has become a place where young people their age have suddenly and violently come face to face with death. Office buildings and other public places such as malls are now perceived as potential terrorist targets. The sound of airplanes overhead is no longer comforting. In addition, every year suicide and accidents snuff out the lives of teens in our communities or those nearby. And many teens have lost loved ones to death due to disease, accident, or old age.

A significant majority of teens also wonder why there is so much suffering in this world. This issue is particularly worrisome for females, with 89% stating they sometimes broach the subject. The news media bring sensational stories of suffering to our living rooms, and those who do not let themselves become desensitized to the violence often feel helpless and question the injustice. For others, personal suffering or that of family or friends heightens their concern.

Almost three in every four teens are asking, "How can I experience happiness?" Although these teens have more money to spend than previous generations and continue to use drugs and alcohol, they are discovering that these do not lead to true happiness. But they're still confused about what experiences *will* lead to happiness.

Just as many teens are contemplating the purpose of life. As teens look forward to the future, they ask, "What will I do with the rest of my life?" The question of purpose naturally follows (and not just for philosophy students).

These are key issues that youth workers need to take seriously.

## Self-Esteem

Volumes have been written on the self-esteem of teenagers, and the survey attempted to quantify it. Surprisingly, 96% of respondents stated that the phrase "I am a good person" described them "fairly well" or "very well." In addition, the vast majority of teens believe they possess a number of good qualities and are well liked. One reason teens have such good self-esteem is that both parents and schools are on the same philosophical page – the school of Romanticism. Our culture teaches students that there are no bad people. We all are good.

Stephen Glenn has studied self-esteem and considers it a "catch-all" phrase for at least two psychological states: exogenous and endogenous self-esteem.[3]

Glenn is concerned that too much self-esteem comes from outside sources. He calls this kind of self-esteem "exogenous." Teenagers have received gold stars that indicate they are good people. This type of "feeling good" produces teens who are people-pleasers. It's like being in a hot-air balloon: You stay afloat as long as you are still connected to the source of hot air, but take that source away, and you come crashing down. Exogenous self-esteem can cheat you: If you chase after the end product – encouragement – without concern for the means by which you get it, you may never make the link between behaviour and reward.

The other source of self-esteem Glenn calls "endogenous": it comes from within, where there is a realistic understanding of self. Challenges are met. Goals are reached. Mistakes are part of the process. Growth happens. People whose self-esteem has grown from within understand their gifts, strengths, and weaknesses, and feel good about their unique mix. "Parents and teachers must ensure that the self-esteem of children is firmly rooted in reality." Glenn writes. "It must be built on a foundation of genuine competence, both academically and socially as well as the ability to personally resolve problems and overcome obstacles. True self-esteem also reflects the development of positive relationships and a sense that one is a contributing member of the community."[4] Many Olympic athletes compete to grow in their abilities and measure themselves against personal goals. Their self-esteem is not based on whether they win a medal. Programs such as Outward Bound also bolster this kind of self-esteem, as participants discover they can do things than they would never have expected.

TABLE 8.4 **Self-Image of Teens Nationally and by Gender**

(% indicating describes them "Very Well" or "Fairly Well")

|  | Nationally | Males | Females |
|---|---|---|---|
| I am a good person. | 96 | 96 | 96 |
| I am well liked. | 93 | 94 | 92 |
| I have a number of good qualities. | 92 | 93 | 91 |
| I can do most things well. | 82 | 87 | 77 |
| I am good-looking | 75 | 79 | 72 |
| I have lots of confidence. | 71 | 79 | 63 |

*Bibby, PTC 2000 data set*

Looking back at Table 8.4, it becomes clear that the great majority of teens believe they are good people, are well-liked, and have many good qualities. But teens are more concerned about their looks and confidence level than they are about their basic self-worth. Let's sharpen our focus here, to look only at "very well" respondents. Only 14% of teenage girls and 22% of teenage boys said a description of themselves as good-looking fit them "very well." And only 20% of teenage girls and 32% of teenage boys said the phrase "I have confidence" fit them "very well." Significant numbers of teens (especially females) lack confidence and/or view their looks as deficient in some way. This ought to be a key concern in youth work.

## Personal Pain

The survey also tapped the issue of personal pain by asking teens to reflect on the degree to which they were aware of a close friend encountering a range of problems. (See Table 8.5.) One caution in interpreting these findings: The numbers listed below cannot be used to extrapolate how many teens encounter personal pain. The close friend of one respondent may be the close friend of another. On the other hand, some teens who experience personal pain may be entirely alone.

TABLE 8.5 **Personal Pain**

"A close friend of mind has experienced…"
(% responding "Yes")

|  | Nationally | Males | Females |
| --- | --- | --- | --- |
| Severe depression | 48 | 39 | 57 |
| A serious drug/alcohol problem | 46 | 44 | 49 |
| Attempted suicide | 41 | 31 | 50 |
| Physical abuse at school | 32 | 39 | 25 |
| Physical abuse at home | 31 | 25 | 37 |
| Sexual abuse | 26 | 18 | 32 |
| Gang violence | 24 | 28 | 21 |

Bibby, Canada's Teens, 2001: 82, 95

These statistics point to the sobering reality that all is not well for certain youth. Violence, depression, addiction, and abuse are dampening the quality of life of many teens.

## One of the Non-Issues

As much as it is crucial to know what teens worry about, it is equally important to understand what they feel least concerned about. Near the bottom of the list comes sex. (I can hear you say teens should be more concerned about it.) Despite what we think, teens do not spend every waking minute thinking about sex. A young woman came up to talk to me after a weekend retreat. She thanked me for not spending all the whole time talking about sex. She said, "It's important to know about, and all, but every year every speaker they bring in always talks about sex the whole weekend. There is a lot more to our lives than sex."

# Why Is This the Case?

## Safety

On the surface, students' increased concern about safety has its roots in the violent events of the past five years and the media's feeding frenzy over them. But that doesn't tell the whole story. Some teens do not feel safe in their schools and in society more generally. The school environment Patricia Hersch entered, for example, had an "attitude that often reeks with the threat of real violence."[5] The bullies from elementary school do not always go away in high school. A growing number of teens feel the need to carry weapons or walk in pairs or groups for safety. Most university and college campuses now have safe-walk programs.

Actual violence is compounded by putdowns and ever-present verbal abuse. Much of teen culture today promotes a culture of mockery. MTV's *Beavis and Butthead* mocks the station's own music videos; *South Park* chews up everybody; some television sitcoms are extended mock-fests. At a recent teachers' conference, one of the main sessions was on how to handle mocking teenagers. As they rush to find friendship clans, teens mock others to avoid being mocked themselves. Mocking is sometimes a sign of membership in the clan. There is a feeling of euphoria in putting down a person outside of your tribe in such a way that the people in your group all "get it." This adds to group cohesion and reminds everyone that you are "in." In one-on-one conversation with a teen, the mocking falls away – it usually has meaning only in the group.

Teens can be brutal to each other, to parents, to anyone who is seen as outside the group. The March 19, 2001, issue of *Time* magazine pointed to mocking as one of the major reasons for physical violence. Teens who are picked on are beginning to retaliate. Mocking back would mean nothing, because they do not have the necessary acceptance in a group. With no way of verbal retaliation, students sometimes lash out physically.

> If you bump into a desk and bruise your leg you don't have to do anything about it. It will heal itself. But when people get put down that is a pain that goes right to the core of who we are as people.... One of the greatest disservices that has happened to us in the last forty years is we have lost our respect for people.

When we hurt people in that way, that pain doesn't heal itself automatically and if we get enough pain and we get angry enough, and ...we keep stuffing it down inside ourselves, we set ourselves up for an explosive moment.[6]

Adults need to be sensitive to the fact that serious emotional abuse is happening on a daily basis in some of our schools at a far higher level than anything they themselves experienced.

Sexual harassment is also a reality in our schools. "In June of 1993, the American Association of University Women had released *Hostile Hallways: The AAUW Survey on Sexual Harassment in America's Schools*, to a blaze of publicity. The report stated that four of five eighth- through eleventh-graders had experienced some form of sexual harassment in their school life."[7] Just hang out at a local high school for any length of time and you will see the butt-slapping and physical pushing (à la martial arts) and hear the gender slurs.

## School/Future Pressures

Teens are very concerned about school pressures. Teenagers have just moved from elementary school, where classes were prescribed for them, to high school, where they can choose courses and activities. With choice comes pressure: whatever courses they choose now could limit their choices in the future. The choice of a technical, math, science, or art class may influence the type of college they can attend. And if high-school marks slip, so does the chance for scholarships and admission to preferred schools.

The underlying fear that drives all this pressure is that if they make the wrong choices, they will limit their career options. Although most people now change careers several times during their lifetime, teens are led to believe that they need to choose their professional identity in high school and stick to it forever. Schools run personality tests and draw up lists of possible professions. Students believe in the results of these tests as if they are visions from a crystal ball, even if the tests recommend careers they may not really want. Parents' high expectations can add to this pressure, particularly if parents are paying for part of the ride. Sometimes parental input is more like a pointed gun than an expectation. A Chinese student told me that in his Asian community the only three possibilities for a future profession were doctor, lawyer, or business person. In his words, "All other jobs are seen as failures." No wonder the future scares the life out of many teenagers.

In my work with teens I have noticed a pattern. First, teens chew on ideas about their future, but do not really talk about it. Next, they open up and tell someone what they may try as a profession. They may drop a casual comment, for example, "I visited my brother who is an ambulance driver. It looks pretty cool." At this point they are looking for feedback, for a coveted comment like, "Hey, I think you would be great at something like that." The job options that teens investigate usually have some connection to their experience. One might think about being a cook because he or she performed this task at summer camp. Perhaps another has an uncle who is a police officer. A group of boys who attended the same camp became firefighters because an influential counsellor at that camp was a firefighter. Finally, if teens have an adult connection to their chosen profession, they may actually try it out by visiting the adult's place of work. Teens who do not have this type of help often simply choose a trade or a major at college by random choice.

## Time

Teens really do have less time for themselves than they did when they were children. Adults sometimes forget that every teenager is going through the transition from childhood to adulthood for the first time. Suddenly there is more homework, a widening circle of friends, and continuing school, extracurricular, and family commitments.

Along with newfound freedoms come newfound time constraints. Teens have to learn to say no. (Not that we as adults always excell at this part of life.) Some teens on our leadership team help out another youth group in the area, play on a sports team and feel they are letting their friends down if they don't hang out until late at night. My young friends feel stressed and pressured to do it all. Only a few years ago Tonka trucks were their major concern.

## Ultimate Questions

Visit any high school after a teen has died in a car accident. Groups huddle, crying, in the hallways. Some of these teens may never even have met the victim. At the funeral, if there is an open microphone, weeping teens will stand up to say, "I never knew this person, but...." They will talk about how this death makes them feel. Death is like a slap in the face, waking them up to their own mortality. With the media highlighting teen suicide and school shootings, teens now have even more reason to think about the ultimate question of what lies beyond the grave.

In the teenage years, expanded mental abilities make people start asking ultimate questions. According to Jean Piaget, world renowned for his study of cognitive development in children, at the age of eleven or twelve, children begin to experience "formal operational thought," which he describes as the ability to "mentally execute possible actions on objects and be able to reflect on these operations in the absence of the objects which are replaced by pure propositions. This reflection power is raised to the second power."[8] Whereas younger children are capable only of limited reflection on things outside their experience, teens are eager to exercise their newly acquired reflective abilities, and are beginning to generalize and idealize. These mental skills, which begin in early adolescence, are honed in mid to late adolescence. I have seen students who are interested in earning stars for "right answers" in Grade 5 beginning to ask questions concerning the origins of evil in Grade 9.

I experienced what Piaget termed "reflection power raised to the second power" while at a retreat. A girl in Grade 9 was complaining of headaches. The cause seemed to be more mental than physical. While on her way to the retreat, she looked over, saw someone in another car looking at her, and realized that she was just a "player" in the other person's world. She tried to understand our positions relative to each other in a larger world and got a headache from the enormity of the possibilities in the idea.

A teen reflects philosophically on life even more than the average adult. Asking ultimate questions – what their purpose is in life or why there is so much evil in the world – is a normal cognitive stage that teenagers must go through.

## Confidence

Put any of us on stage and ask us how confident we feel. Even after two decades of practice, I get a bit shaky being up there. Many teenagers feel they are onstage twenty-four hours a day, seven days a week. Once, when I was waiting for my family to finish shopping, I strolled by the local high school to observe my favourite group of people. The students were just leaving school for the day. Many individuals were very loud – sometimes shouting someone's name from across the street, sometimes dancing around, looking for group approval. Standing back and observing all the theatrics, it was easy for me to see adolescents feel that all eyes are on them. A college student of mine commented in a self-evaluation of his adolescence, "There was no doubt that I considered myself to be on 'stage' twenty-four hours a day. I felt tremendous pressure to be something that was not my natural self."

Adolescents quickly pick up the language of each new fad. As they look at their changing faces in the mirror, they realize that their peers are also looking at them, measuring them against media standards. Corporations create ever-changing teen styles to augment comparisons between what is new and what is out. Teen magazines such as *Seventeen* flaunt the newest styles with airbrushed-perfect models, who become standards against which readers judge their friends and themselves.

Erik Erikson observes that the comparison of self with others, with an ideal image as a yardstick, is a part of identity formation:

> Identity formation employs a process of simultaneous reflection and observation, a process taking place on all levels of mental functioning, by which the individual judges himself in the light of what he perceives to be the way in which others judge him in comparison to themselves and to a typology significant to them; while he judges their way of judging him in light of how he perceives himself in comparison to them and to types that have become relevant to him.[9]

Media and marketers exacerbate this process by constantly changing what adolescents "should" look like. Light jeans, dark jeans, cargo pants, and bellbottoms float in and out of style. As a result, teenagers constantly wonder what others are thinking of them. They are magnets to any metal filing of comment. No wonder their confidence gets beaten down at times.

# What Does This Mean for Youth Work?

## Create Places of Safety

The knowledge that normal life does not provide safety for teens gives us a tremendous opportunity. Steve Brown, my pastoral partner, works with many students who are not from church backgrounds. He relates this story: "Shortly after the tragedy in Littleton, we asked the high-school students at our youth outreach to name one place where they felt loved, accepted, and safe. Immediately, several students answered, 'not at school.' A number of others quickly answered, 'not at home.' After a few more seconds of reflection, one student after another said that the one place they felt loved, accepted, and safe was at RIOT – our weekly outreach. We were reminded that in the heavy seas of their young lives, teenagers desperately need youth ministries to be break-walls and beacons of love, acceptance, and security."

We have had to work hard to make our group a place of safety. We've had to ask teens to leave because they were carrying knives or dealing drugs. Some people may think it is not "nice" to tell students to leave. But it can be done in a kind, respectful but firm way that lets them know that their behaviour is not welcome in our safe place. The other students applaud our efforts. A safety pledge floating in cyberspace is being adopted in some schools:

1. I pledge to reach out to those who don't fit in.
2. I pledge to hang with those who feel like outcasts.
3. I pledge to share with my teachers and parents any plans of violence I have heard about.
4. I pledge to tell school authorities of anyone in my school carrying a weapon.
5. I pledge to never carry a weapon to school.
6. I pledge to pray for my school, my teachers and others students daily.

Many of us may not have to deal with physical safety issues, but will need to take a firm stand against verbal abuse. Kids need to be told regularly to say only things that build up (Eph 4:29). We must take an active role in letting kids know we do not tolerate put-downs. For every student who thinks we are being too strict, ten more will stay, breathing a sigh of relief at having found a place of safety from the verbal onslaught.

Building such places of safety means not only keeping the negative comments away, but looking for ways to build students up. In our group, we regularly hold an "encouragement circle." During this activity, each student in turn must sit quietly while the others tell him or her positive things they see in his or her life. We also have an "encouragement tub," into which students place encouraging notes they have written. The encouragement coordinator passes the notes out at the end of the night.

In an affluent area where I pastored, the teen group included a bunch of guys whose life was football. They wore their jerseys to youth meetings, talked about the games, and put football stickers on everything they owned (and on some things they didn't own). One youth night, Potsy (so nicknamed for obvious reasons), a well-respected football player, attended. In the eyes of the guys he had it all – he got drunk and smoked up every weekend, slept around, and was very good at football. When our guys saw him arrive at youth group, they all hid. They all thought, "Oh, man, I hope he doesn't catch me here!" That night we had an encouragement circle. Afterwards, Potsy was all smiles. Instead of thinking that youth group was "lame," he asked if we could call him by his real name there and if he could come out again. He told me that the football locker room was not a safe place, but at this youth group he had found a place of real acceptance. Later that year he became a Christian, and the rest of the football guys in our group looked at their faith with fresh perspective. If their hero, who had everything they secretly desired, thought that Christ was "a good deal," they too would look more closely at Christianity. I realized then that encouragement creates safety for the entire group.

## Show Teens God's Hand in Their Future

We can make a big difference to teens as they face the future. As they look for meaningful work, we can help give perspective and encouragement. Even more than previous generations, teens' careers will have great fluidity, and they must define themselves by more than just what they do to earn money. Our job is to help teenagers to see how God has "wired" them, what gifts God has given them to help them serve others.

I love to expose students to authentic people of faith, people who are living out their faith in secular jobs. They see a model of behaviour they will remember for a lifetime. My buddy who owns a garage says "God bless you" to customers, leaves room for conversations about God with his mechanics, gives out worship CDs to those who have a lot of work done on their vehicles, and gives people of little means a break on their bills. When I take teens to visit him, they come away with a good sense of what it means to be a Christian in the secular marketplace.

Students are often frightened of the future simply because they believe they have to face it alone. Parents and school friends won't be there to hold their hands on the job. We must show them that they are never alone: God has promised to travel the roads of the future with us.

I attended a leadership training camp one summer during my college days. During one of our first activities, I was given a map and a compass and was told to lead the entire group to the next food drop-off point. I never had tried my hand at orienteering before, but I used the compass to find the right heading and tentatively moved along, with a whole group of college guys slowly shuffling in a line behind me. After some time, the guide accompanying us told me to take a setting of a tree in the distance and run there to take my next setting. From the guide's show of confidence in me, the whole group was headed in the right direction and we knew we would make it to the food drop-off point before sunset.

I believe God has a compass setting for each of us. He taps us on the shoulder to show us our next step. If we prove faithful, he gradually gives us more to do and he continues to guide us. Teens often want to know God's plan for their entire lives. I encourage them to move toward the heading they have now and to wait for the next one to come into view.

## Model Good Time Leadership

Adults are stressed for time and unwittingly model this for teens. As one youth pastor told me, "My youth began equating busyness with godliness, because they were following my example." If we want to help our youth to manage time, some of us need to make some significant changes in the way we manage our own time.

Some youth groups encourage teems to get day planners and keep to-do lists. Some teens need this! There is a lot of wasted time in their day-to-day lives. There is a big difference between real recreation and misused time. An all-nighter of computer games, for instance, leaves most teens feeling empty and wasted. Day planners can help them to see the big picture of how much (or little) time they've been given to work with. We teach teens, "If my private world is in order, it is because I have begun to seal the 'time leaks' and allocate my productive hours in the light of my capabilities, my limits, and my priorities."[10]

Even more important than time management is time leadership, which asks the question "Are we headed in the right direction?" It is possible to travel quickly and efficiently in a wrong direction. As the saying goes, "The enemy of the best is not the bad, but the good."

Time leadership asks students why they are on this planet. During our Excalibur leadership training program, students ask themselves questions like "What would I want people to say about me at my funeral?"; "What treasures in heaven would I like to have?"; "How has God wired me, specifically, with my gifts, calling, and personality?" After some thought, students write life mission statements – starting points for their direction in life. A twenty-year-old made up this statement: "To influence others to become influencers themselves in order to systematically increase the size of God's family." Did this help focus this young man's life? Absolutely. He now has the power to say no to activities that will waste his time because they don't further the achievement of his life mission. We often have the strength to say no only when a bigger YES burns in our souls.

As students watch us set goals in each of our roles and then schedule them into our year, they will do the same. One of my dreams is to influence this next generation. I would like to be known for that when I die. To accomplish this, I need to be "a man after God's heart." To fulfill that role, I have set myself goals, including a several-day retreat in which I go away to read, write in my journal, and reflect with God. I schedule this retreat in my Day Timer. I have taken control of my time. This is time leadership. Observing me, a sixteen-year-old girl tried something similar and came back after a day away just hopping with excitement in her newfound direction.

One ancient practice that has caught the imagination of teenagers is that of Sabbath rest. I am not talking about the "do-nothing" teaching of thirty years ago. I remember those days, when some people slept on couches while an unprivileged few did the dishes. I am talking about a Sabbath where teens do what God did on the seventh day: He reflected, evaluated, and said it was good. I just talked to a student who had taken an afternoon off to hang out at the park and write about her week in her journal. She was rested and was just about jumping to get started on her new week. Dr. Richard A. Swenson gives several prescriptions for calming the activity storm. Here are some of them: "Consider doing ten per cent less, not more. Periodically prune away activities. Limit long-term commitments. Work to maintain balance – an unexamined life will drift toward imbalance. Remember who it is that gets things done. God can do in twenty minutes what it takes us twenty years to do. Is it busyness that moves mountains...or faith?"[11]

## Discuss Ultimate Questions

Postmodernism has moved us away from logic and "answers" and toward subjective experience. Because of this, many youth workers stay away from any kind of "question answering" ministry. But teens, developmentally, are in the "metaphysical" stage: they want to explore the questions of the ages. I occasionally talk to student groups about reasons to believe in God. They eat this topic up, with questions and comments and many sighs of relief. Students often say they have never heard anyone talk about these things before.

In our culture, we have left apologetics behind, but it is very important to those coming of age. We may not have rock-solid answers, but neither have we been unthinking the last 2,000 years. We have, in fact, thought about questions such as "How can there be a God that is loving and active when there is so much suffering in the world?" "Why is Jesus so important?" "Don't all religions teach basically the same things?"[12] These questions will likely not be asked in a secular classroom, so we need to address them.

The question of what happens after death is a particular area of expertise for us. Who else will speak about this if we do not? We have the distinct advantage of having quotations from someone who has fully died and come alive again – Jesus. I think many of us are uncomfortable talking about death. C.S. Lewis said there are only three things to do with death: fear it, ignore it, or live in light of it. Our culture hides death under the banner of the first two responses. But we youth workers have the wonderful opportunity to help students understand their mortality and face the subject of death and the world that is yet to come.

## Help Teens Grow in Confidence

Youth workers have a great opportunity to set students up for success! Real challenges, met with our help, will build lasting self-esteem and confidence. I lead a three-weekend leadership-training course called Excalibur Leadership Training. On one such weekend, two of the students came from another church's youth group. We gave them some skills, and they went back to their group and planned an event that thirty-six kids attended. Were they pumped? Were they more confident? You bet! Confidence-building can be as easy as taking the time for good training, giving constructive oversight, and giving teens the opportunity to run with the ball.

Students have internal radar that can sense confidence in others. They flock to people with confidence. They are also very sensitive to "fakes" – those who appear confident, but don't have anything inside that matches the "store window". There are few greater compliments than for a teenager to call you "real."

Writing about modelling, Kohlberg observes that teens imitate behaviour that stimulates their curiosity, makes them yearn to explore more, and instills a desire for mastery. When an adult performs in a way that is interesting or exemplifies mastery, teens want to model that behaviour. We youth leaders need to display our competencies, particularly in our spiritual lives. If we stand out as unusual, students will notice our models of positive spiritual life. If we show love to a student, along with a set of competencies, they will follow. Adult modelling is a powerful influence to those who are looking for confidence and are open to input.

Finally, this old pattern is still helpful in giving students confidence: I do, you watch; you do, I watch; you do.

## To Do Today

- Teach your students what the book of Proverbs says about mocking.
- Hold an open house youth group meeting in the event that a student is killed in an accident in your area. Be prepared to answer the question, "What happens after I die?"
- Turn your youth group into a safety zone from physical and emotional hurt. One youth group created and posted signs with the word "mock" and the internationally recognized red circle with a slash through it: "You are entering a no-mock zone."
- Have your students finish the statement "The place I feel most safe is ____."
- Invite various professions into your youth group to talk about what they do and – even more important – who they are within and outside of their jobs.
- Offer a personality test like the Myers-Briggs type indicator to help teens understand whether they are introverts or extroverts and so on.
- Grab your Day Timer and schedule an event that your student leaders can run (or you can run with them) to build confidence. If you don't have a leadership team, open up the opportunity to anyone who wants to try.
- Schedule in an encouragement circle with your youth group this week. Develop encouragement mailboxes with the names of your students on them, or an encouragement bucket.
- Take out your annual calendar now and plan several days when teens can sign up to follow around some of your faith stars at their places of work. Choose your adult models well, and cue them to talk about how they live their faith out loud in a secular environment.

- Proclaim a Sabbath experiment for your youth group. Encourage them to spend an afternoon away from the usual distractions to pray, read, and write in a journal. Then have them come back and discuss what that experience did for them.
- Take your youth group to a ropes course. Before each event, help them set some personal goals for what they want to achieve.

# CHAPTER NINE
# Romancing Risk

I t was the first few weeks into my job as a youth pastor in Iowa. A bunch of students told me that they were going swimming in the Mississippi. Sounded good to me. I wanted to make a good impression, so I chimed, "Count me in!" When we arrived at the river, the students climbed out of the cars and ran to this huge metal structure, a "coal dock," rusty from years of disuse. The teens used this loading platform as a diving platform. I saw one teen fly over the edge, screaming. I, with typical adult caution, crawled on my soft belly to peer down at the river. My eyes focused on the tiny head of the teen some fifty feet below me. He screamed, "What a rush! Come on in." As all the teens, one by one, jumped over the edge. I contemplated how strange a picture this would be if these were middle-aged people jumping to their near deaths. That day I realized just how much risk is a "teen thing." (By the way, I did suck in my belly and jump.)

Teen skateboarders surf the urban landscape with abandon of life and limb, executing "switch-stance, kick-flip, nose wheelies" or "front-side, heel-flip, nose-slides." The more dangerous the move – and the greater the wipeout – the more status they gain. Skateboarders wear their scars as badges of honour.

A group of nineteen-year-olds in my church shared pictures with me of their skydiving trip, while other youth looked on with true envy. Some teens try extreme sports and midway rides. Others engage in unprotected sex, run away to the inner city, or smoke. Teens romance danger to maximize the experience.

Risk-taking does not go against the desire for safety we talked about in the last chapter. This risk-taking centres on the type of limits teens themselves can tackle. The question of "Who am I?" begs the question for teens, what limits can I take? This is risk-taking. The issues of safety are risky things that come from outside the person. The need for teens to feel safe centres around the desire for them to have the space and freedom to take their own risks.

## Survey Says: Teens Crave Excitement

Ninety-two per cent of teens view excitement as "very important" or "somewhat important." Gender differences are small: a slightly greater number of males (58%) place a high value on excitement than do females (55%). Adults, however, are less enthralled. We like excitement, but as we age, we want it to come in doses we can easily recover from. By our senior years, very few of us are turned on by excitement at all.

TABLE 9.1 **Excitement: An Intergenerational Comparison**

(% viewing as "very important")

| |
|---|
| Teens — 57 |
| Young Adults — 43 |
| Parents — 26 |
| Grandparents — 19 |

*Source: Canada's Teens, 2001: 230*

Forty-one per cent of those teens who claim to be presently engaging in sex state that the risk of AIDS has not changed their sexual habits. This is a life-or-death kind of risk – the stakes are very high.

Almost one-quarter of the teen population smoke cigarettes weekly. This figure is down slightly from young adults, but is still very high. Approximately the same percentage of adults smoke cigarettes weekly. Knowing that smoking is so addictive, one wonders how many of these adults began smoking as teens. Some believe smoking can be used as a marker for other high-risk behaviour. For example, our survey shows a moderate correlation between teen cigarette smoking and teen sexual activity: Of those teens who never smoke, 64% are still virgins; among teens who smoke weekly, 78% have also engaged in sex. One psychologist I spoke to explained that if he could keep students from smoking, he could save them from many other high-risk behaviours.

Adolescent psychiatrist Lynn Ponton reminds us that risk is a fact of teen life: "In my work two things have remained absolutely clear over the years: adolescents are going to take risks, and most parents of adolescents are terrified about this. In 1995, when the Carnegie Institute published its findings on youth and risk, its report suggested that American youths today are at greater risk because they take more risks and are exposed to even more opportunities for dangerous risk than at any other time in American history."[1]

## Why Is This the Case?

Many factors contribute to a teenager's openness to risky behaviour. Personal or family history plays a role, as do developmental pressures. We cannot paint all situations with one brush, but let's examine some common reasons behind teens' romance with risk.

In *Identity, Youth and Crisis*, American psychologist Erik Erikson writes that adolescents "try on" identities, searching to find the best fit. This search often involves leaps of change – and any great change involves risk. Risk feels seductive, exciting, and adult-like.

Psychologist David Elkind says adolescents are not adept in distinguishing between transient and abiding events: that is, what will be quickly forgotten and what has long-term effects. If a teenager gets teased for tripping over a doorjamb, she may worry that her friends will remember that image forever: "I'll just die if I see them again – they will be talking about what a fool I made of myself." On the other hand, the same teen may get a tattoo without seriously thinking through the forever implications of it.

Elkind also observed that adolescents have trouble distinguishing between the universal and the particular. In their minds, what applies to others (universally in adult minds) may not apply particularly to them. Elkind names this tendency the "personal fable."[2] In teens' minds, drugs that are additive will not affect them. More than one teen has said, "Others may get pregnant, but I will not." One day, as I was driving a carload of teens to a retreat, one of the teens asked a friend for a cigarette. I happened to know that this teen did not smoke. I looked back and asked, "What are you doing? You don't smoke, Wallace." He smiled and told me he wanted to try the experience of smoking for the long weekend and then he would stop. I tried to tell him that nicotine is an additive drug. He smiled with the confidence of more years than he had experienced and told me that it wouldn't hook him.

Some adolescent risk-taking simply stems from lack of experience. In the attempt to "be adult," teens sometimes go places and participate in activities without realizing the huge risk involved. They do not want to accept advice from adults because it hearkens back to childhood days, when they were told what to do. A girl I know was invited to a keg party, which was being held out in a forest. Her parents begged her not to go.

She assured them that she knew the people at the party well. They tried to tell her that people's behaviour changes when they are drunk. I was called in later, when they found out that one of her "friends" had raped her. As Dr. Ponton writes, "Teens will put themselves in life-threatening situations with little knowledge about how they got there or how to help themselves."[3] We must help teenagers by encouraging them to gain experience in lower-risk activities that do not hold lifelong consequences.

As they do for so many aspects of adolescent life, the media capitalize on teen risk-taking tendencies. The adventures and love affairs on movie and television screens are so much brighter and bolder than those in real life. Teens are looking for new experiences. As children they understood life through the concrete situations they experienced. Now, as teenagers, they are open to understanding life in ideal ways. Who are their guides? The Yoda of life experience is often the latest movie or television show. Dr. Ponton writes that teens sometimes see ideal situations on television and do not yet have the life experience to know that some of these stories aren't even possible. She says, "I worry about the impact of the fantasy families that...kids watch on television."[4] We do, too.

# What Does This Mean for Youth Work?

## Provide Opportunities for Positive Risk-Taking

Risk-taking is a natural activity for teens. From their perspective, they are walking into the great unknown of adult life. Any kind of journey to the unknown involves risk. If teens do not take risky steps, they will be stunted in their natural growth.

If our teens want to experience risk, the natural question is, how risky are the experiences in your church? We believe youth groups need to be risky in mission, risky in relationships, risky in fun. In one seminary class I teach, I ask who the competition is for youth groups. Some students answer "Last Baptist down the street" or "The cults across town." Wrong! Think of the analogy of eating. The competition for Taco Bell is another fast-food restaurant or a home-cooked meal. The competition for a youth group or campus club is anything kids like to do with their free time: television, movies, sports teams, "vegging." Now let's ask the question again. How risky is the experience at your group?

I spoke to leaders at one national Christian youth organization who wondered why their attendance was dropping. Just before I got up to speak they made a big announcement about their year-end "highlight" activity. They were going bowling. Wow, what excitement and risk! I could see that the teens at this banquet were underwhelmed.

How can we work together to provide opportunities for positive risk-taking? Many Christian camps allow for everything from parasailing to zip lines to rock diving. The students eat it up. The following excerpt comes from Lydia, a teen who annually heads to the mountains for a horseback wilderness camp. I asked her why she risks via camping. Here are her words:

> Some of the best days of my life have been spent taking risks at camp. I remember riding bareback down a mountain. We weren't following a trail. The ride was really, really steep, and could have been very dangerous had one of the horses slipped or if one of the riders had fallen off. It was an adventure, though; we were doing something new; something different! Another thing about risk is that it is just plain fun. I remember swimming on horse-back in a river. Sure, there were dangers – but it was fun! That was six years ago and I still look back at it with fond memories. Another factor in risk is pride. I'm proud to say that I have gone ten days in the bush with no running water, power, or modern conveniences. I'm proud that I have ridden where hardly any-one else has. I'm proud that I have pushed until I have made it to the top of a mountain.

In the games we play, in the ministry we do, risk adds the spice that teens yearn for.

Christians have been taking risks for centuries in their missions. Large numbers of teenagers travel around the globe every summer to risk their time, their money, their health, and their relationships back home to go and make a difference in a new culture. According to the survey, an incredible 72% of teenagers expected to travel extensively outside of their country in the years to come.

Missions can be good for the world, but they may have the most meaning for the teens themselves. Dave, a fifteen-year-old from Abbotsford, British Columbia, is one such example. At the suggestion of a twenty-three-year-old camp director he knew, Dave spent four weeks teaching mountain biking at a Latvian camp last year. He brought along $3,000 worth of BMX bikes he and his church had obtained through fundraising. Here are some of Dave's comments about his trip.

When I had the chance, I decided to take it – even though I had a fear of not knowing the language and being in a different culture – because I like working with children. If I had stayed home last summer I would have worked, mountain biked, and waterskied. [In Latvia] you are helping a little kid have fun. It's way more relaxed. It's easier to be a Christian there, not the same distractions like TV, what you look like, how much money you have. You can use any talent to serve God. I love mountain biking. It's my hobby. Whatever talents you have, God can use. When you are there, it is so much fun! Afterwards you don't even notice that you missed the money. I came back more thankful for what we have here. We have so much.

Reflecting on her time as a disaster consultant, Dr. Ponton points out, "I made some interesting observations. Teens in the disaster-affected areas who were allowed, even encouraged, to participate in the exhausting, yet at times exhilarating, disaster work were less likely to get involved in risky behavior."[5] One family in my church sent their daughter on several missions trips throughout her teen years. They highly recommend it, saying the experience builds responsibility in raising money, broadens horizons as other cultures are experienced, and satisfies the teen desire for risk. Even riding a roller coaster doesn't match up to building an orphanage in the tropics.

Teens do not have to travel thousands of miles for this type of experience. Inner-city ministry involves a great deal of risk. Participating in a soup kitchen can be gruelling. I have seen students pushed to their limits by handing out lunches on the street. But after one such experience, a dating couple started to hand out lunches on their own to the street people of our city, choosing the experience of ministry over watching another video in their parents' basement.

One of the riskiest adventures of life is public speaking. What a great risk, to tell the life story of how God works in your life! We take teenagers on a leadership course in which they learn to share a section of their life story in front of their peers. Before these talks, the teens are more nervous than I have ever seen them. Speaking in public ranks right up there with skydiving on the scary-meter.

Some teens romance risk because they want to experience as much as possible. Teens trust their own experience. There is so much information out there, experience becomes the quick refiner of "what works." In teens' minds, the experts are not necessarily to be trusted. In the survey, teens were asked where they received their moral information. Nearly half indicated it was from personal factors. Bibby concludes, "Young people are increasingly interpreting values and morality in a very personal, as opposed to communal, sense."[6] A pastor or priest can tell teens what is right or wrong, but unless personal experience backs up the information, teens are not going to buy it.

Not too many years ago, teens liked to be spectators – spectators at concerts, spectators in front of the television. Now, being a spectator is boring to them. They want to experience more, to participate in moshing at concerts, to crawling inside the screen and create their own Web sites.

In the biblical world risk has another name. Picture the disciples in the storm-tossed fishing boat. Jesus comes walking across the water to them. What would a teen in that boat do? Probably call out, "Hey, can I try that too?" and step out of the boat. Picture the outnumbered Israelites lined up in battle gear, listening to a huge, experienced warrior dare anyone to take him on in battle, the visible notches on his belt reminding them of those who have tried and failed. What would a teen say in such a situation? "Hey, let me take him on. I've killed things with a slingshot before!" The biblical record reminds us that faith and risk-taking often go hand in hand. If we have all of life figured out and never run any real risk, can we call our acts faith? I don't think so.

Teens have a unique role to play in our local churches – reminding us to take risk. They can be a stimulant to us to take faith-risks, to live faith in radical ways. When Jesus came into town, those who were filled with faith were willing to take the risk of quitting their jobs, closing up their houses, and following him. As theologian Rikk Watts says: "Like Jesus, challenge teens with giving themselves to something beyond themselves. This is a challenge that is risk-taking...the forming of a revolutionary movement that actually engages the mind and tries to change the way people live!"[7]

Teens need to see more adults willing to take faith-risks. Bibby's survey found that only 20% of adults are willing to talk about their faith to others in their religious group.[8] We adults need courage here. We can model what it means to take the risk of sharing our faith or giving to the poor more than we have saved as surplus. Take risks in praying for someone when it is needed, right there, out loud. Take risks in sharing faith, not shying away when asked about it.

We have noticed over the years that the adult heroes in many youth groups are those who live their faith in radical ways, giving teenagers examples of healthy risk-taking. If risk is a normal part of becoming an adult, we need to ask how the church and parents can work together to make positive risk-taking possible.

## To Do Today

- Plan a retreat at a camp that has a ropes course, climbing wall, horseback riding, a zip line, etc. Ask the director to have camp staff ready to take the entire group through the risky adventure.
- Prepare your next series of devotionals on risk-takers in the Bible. The lives of David, Daniel, Esther, or Paul may be good places to start.
- Plan a missions trip to another culture. Get in touch with some missionaries that your church/denomination supports and e-mail them to see if they have a project your group could participate in. As part of your trip, fundraise above and beyond the project to bless your cross-cultural hosts.
- Ask to put on a Sunday morning youth service at your church. Have the teens give speeches about what God is doing in their lives. Have a few of them give a message on living lives of faith. Let them fulfill their roles in the church as stirrers of risk.
- Write an encouragement note to a youth or youth leader who is "living on the edge." Remind the person how important their role is in the group.
- Encourage your teens to get involved in a Christian group in their high schools, where it is very risky to live out faith.
- Plan a service project that blesses an inner-city area near you. Collect food for a food bank, clean up a park, or provide a children's program for a housing complex.

# CHAPTER TEN

# The New Dictionary of Values

The embers were growing low at the bonfire on the last night of youth camp. A guest speaker was pacing around the fire, telling stories of real commitment. The air was so quiet that all you could hear was the crackle of the dry wood. Then the speaker asked for a response from the students: "If you want to tell the rest of the group that you are truly committed to Christ, I want you to get up and throw a faggot on the fire." For some reason, the speaker never quite understood why no one carried through with the request – snickers just made their way around the campfire.

Scene two from the journals of youth ministry legend: A missionary from the jungles of the Amazon had just finished his talk. The time for questions came, and a teen asked what kind of clothes were best when hiking in the rain forest. The missionary told the teens, "Well, anytime you head out in the rain forest you always have to take your rubbers with you." Needless to say, the teens burst out laughing and their minds were not on raingear.

Language changes; it is alive and in constant flux. Since we use language to convey meaning, we need to make sure the words we choose do not get in the way of understanding. The survey showed that some values need to be reworded or our communication will misfire. This is particularly true in the area of our faith. Our culture lost its Christian base so long ago, most non-churched teens I have talked to don't have any idea of Christ's role in Easter or Christmas. Yet many of the values we hope our students will adopt are from Christ. There are specific Christian ideas behind forgiveness and controlling our tongues, but mainstream society does not teach these ideas. Instead, it speaks to the millennials in a language that is quite different. To make a difference in their lives, we need to understand our teenagers' new language of values.

Many people believe we should focus on the problems of teen drug use or violence. We believe these are symptomatic of deeper causes: How teenagers think about what is right and wrong, what they think about their experiences. To understand these root causes, we must look beyond teens' actions into the culture of thought that they are steeped in. This chapter, therefore, is more philosophical than the others. We do not hope to make a serious philosophical argument in the space of one chapter; we hope our observations will help you look beyond what teens do, to ask how their thoughts affect their actions.

## Survey Says: Honesty Is Important, But What Is Honesty?

TABLE 10.1 **Interpersonal Values**

(% viewing as "Very Important")

|  | 2000 | 1984 |
|---|---|---|
| Friendship | 85 | 91 |
| Being loved | 77 | 87 |
| Honesty | 73 | 85 |
| Concern for others | 62 | * |
| Politeness | 58 | 64 |
| Forgiveness | 58 | 66 |
| Working hard | 52 | 69 |
| Generosity | 43 | * |
| Creativity | 42 | * |

* not asked for in the 1984 data

Bibby, Canada's Teens, 2001: 13, 16 and Bibby, PTC 1984 data set

The survey tells us that next to friendship and being loved, which we have examined previously, honesty is the most important interpersonal teen value. I have spoken with many a teen who said of their involvement in certain situations, "At least I was honest." One young woman told me she was pregnant. As she talked about her predicament, she said that at least she was honest about her life. Yet in having sex, she constantly lied to her parents about where she was spending time. Certainly, her definition of honesty is different than how honesty was defined not too many years ago.

### TABLE 10.2 A Peek at Honesty in Action

"A person gives you change for what you have bought. As you walk away, you realize he/she has given you $10 more than you were supposed to receive. What would you be inclined to do?"

(% indicating that answer)

|  | Nationally | Females | Males |
| --- | --- | --- | --- |
| 1. Keep the $10 and keep walking. | 34 | 27 | 41 |
| 2. Go back to return the extra $10. | 35 | 42 | 28 |
| 3. It would depend on factors such as size of the store, whether you knew the salesperson involved, etc. | 31 | 31 | 31 |
| Teens who say honesty is "very important to them" | 73 | 83 | 62 |

*Bibby,* Canada's Teens, *2001: 16, 18*

More and more, values that were cherished as standards only a few years ago are now being stretched to mean different things depending on the situation. In this test case, one-third of the students who were asked whether they would give back a ten-dollar "mistake" replied that it depended on the circumstances. If the store was big, the ten dollars would not really matter to them – no one would get hurt. If the students did not intend to shop at the store again, they did not have any loyalty to the place, so too bad – it was their mistake. If they didn't know the salesperson, they felt it was okay to keep the money. On the other hand, if the salesperson was a friend or someone they might run into again, they would be inclined to give the money back, because the friend would get into trouble if the money in the register didn't match up with the sales.

In all these examples, you may notice that a principle called "honesty," a principle with substance, a spiritual life to it, has lost its meaning. The kids have interwoven feelings and levels of moral reasoning, but "honesty" itself does not play a part in their decisions. Yet 73% of them report that honesty is very important to them!

# Why Is This the Case?

The survey asked what values were important, but did not test what most of those values meant to teens. However, it did test what assumptions teens were likely to make about the meaning of honesty. This test case brings to the foreground some patterns we have noticed in our work with youth that affect how they turn their values into actions. These patterns include the revitalization of values, the filters of friends and freedom, and the feminization of values.

## Revitalization of Values

When asked a question concerning moral views, 65% answered that "everything is relative."[1] Bibby found that "a fifteen-year-old from a small city in Manitoba states the situation succinctly: 'Truth is in the eye of the beholder.'"[2]

Many philosophers describe the relativization of truth.[3] In *Truth Is Stranger Than It Used to Be,* authors Richard Middleton and Brian Walsh relay a joke in which three umpires are talking after a game:

> One says, "There's balls and there's strikes and I call 'em the way they are." Another responds, "There are balls and there's strikes and I call 'em the way I see 'em." The third says, "There's balls and there's strikes, and they ain't nothin' until I call 'em."[4]

In the arena of popular ethics, the first umpire is naive to think there are such things as true balls and true strikes. The second is closer to the way people think today, admitting that truth is seen through fallible eyes. The last umpire is a true relativist in his insistence that the act of calling balls and strikes gives the balls thrown their reality.

The last umpire's way of seeing life is taught in the classroom, at the movies, and through the daily news. Our teenagers have been brought up in an environment in which there is no moral reality except the one people call for themselves. What makes a behaviour right or wrong is the act of calling it so.

Scholarly philosophy is popularized by the media for general readers, who in turn weave their understanding of the philosophy into the fabric of society. Hundreds of years ago, faith was the formational theme for understanding life. In many cases it may have been blind faith, but it was still faith. Now many are catching up with seventeenth-century philosopher René Descartes.

Descartes began his examination of life from the stance of doubt. Because he could cast doubt upon the existence of everything except his own thoughts, he stated, "I think, therefore I am." After Descartes, the idea of starting from a platform of doubt instead of one of faith became a popular way to experience intellectual life. A group of British philosophers called the empiricists emphasized gaining measurable knowledge through the senses. Measurable knowledge meant repeatable scientific experiments, which, when they had similar outcomes on a repeated basis, produced laws. This, too, became part of the public mindset. People, including Christians, doubted anything written about Christianity that could not be explained by the science of the day. Many miracles in the Bible cannot be repeated in a closed, experimental way, and so in many modernists' minds the Bible is parable, not reality. In programs on the History Channel and articles in *Time* magazine, great thinkers wonder who the real Jesus was. They presuppose that Jesus could not have performed miracles because his miracles cannot be proven and repeated. They rejected as inaccurate any part of the biblical record that reports miracles.

Now we have the postmodernists, who have reacted against the modernist faith in the ability to "know" something. Someone in the process of observing nature, for example, is still *involved* with nature; therefore, no one can be truly objective about nature. In the popular take on postmodernism, the possibility of knowing *anything* is in question.[5] This is transferred to ethics: nothing can be known as right or wrong, so every ethical act is a matter of personal faith. For example, a postmodernist may not believe that taking food from a store is inherently "wrong." If you are hungry enough, or if the store is unjust enough, stealing might be justifiable. The only guidance people have lies in what they believe about the ethics of stealing. This is the world in which our teens have been raised.

It is difficult to defend an ethic of pure relativism. If moral truth is housed within each person, a person who feels an entire race needs to be annihilated has an acceptable point of view. If moral truth is housed within each person, being true to oneself could create the most horrible society ever built.

Many philosophers understand moral truths to be socially constructed. The will of the people or the "vote" of society sets what is morally acceptable. Unfortunately, societies sometimes give the "okay" to immoral acts. Many wars are sparked by a desire for genocide that is sanctioned, if not participated in, by the majority of a group of people.

Other philosophers have chosen a type of utilitarianism to guide their ethics. Utilitarianism (sometimes referred to as "the greatest happiness theory"[6]) understands "right" as something that promotes the greatest happiness for the greatest number of people. This is a wonderful ethic, until someone must be asked to choose pain in order to benefit a larger group of people. It's hard to motivate yourself to help the greater good when it comes at a heavy cost to your own happiness.

Humanism, which holds highest what is good for humans, is another popular ethic. But the question "What is good for humans?" is a difficult one. What might seem good in the short-term may have dire consequences in the long-term. And the average teen has difficulty moving from "what is good for me" to "what is good for humans." Although there are teens who behave well out of utilitarian or humanistic motives, many have not found the motivation to higher moral reasoning, and live relativistically.

For many, living ethically in our cultural waters involves "what feels right at the time" – and this may change with the players in a given situation. In these confusing times, teens look at what works for their friends and experiment to see if that ethic may work for them for a time. In our culture, we are exposed to a smorgasbord of beliefs. Christianity is just one of many to take a snippet from. The message many of our teenagers are getting is, all you need to do is be true to yourself.

## The Lens of Friendship

Since teens recognize no transcendent truths, whatever values we talk about take on the colour of their chief interests: friends and freedom. I have asked many teens what they mean when they say that honesty is important. Many describe honesty in relational terms such as "being real." One teen wrote, "Honesty is about loving someone enough to be upfront with them. You love them enough when it means you might lose them because of being straight with them about stuff." Another teen wrote how important total honesty is and then put it in relational terms. "Honesty to me is the absolute truth. Honesty is an essential – often lacking – element in any relationship." Another teen stated, "Honesty is so important to me, I only share it with my friends. It is something that is earned."

In other words, many teens believe a person must be honest to themselves and friends. This type of honesty may not include being honest to a stranger, a parent, or, as in the survey, a corporate store. In my pregnant teen friend's mind, she could be honest to her friends about who she is, yet lie to her parents with no sense of dishonesty.

A dozen teens sitting around a campfire were asked to imagine that, although their parents had told them to go only to one friend's house, they had gone to three friends' houses. If, later that night, their parents asked them how their night was, what would they say? They unanimously replied that they would not mention the other two friends' houses. In addition, they believed it would not be dishonest to omit this information. In other words, they believed they could paint an inaccurate picture of reality and still be honest. If we were to compile a dictionary describing the values of teenagers, the definition of honesty might sound something like this: "Honesty is being totally real with your friends about who you are."

## The Feminization of Interpersonal Values

Every interpersonal value measured by the survey (except creativity, at the bottom of the list) was given more importance by females than by males.

TABLE 10.3 **Interpersonal Values by Gender**

(% viewing as "Very Important")

|  | Males | Females |
| --- | --- | --- |
| Honesty | 62 | 83 |
| Politeness | 51 | 65 |
| Forgiveness | 47 | 67 |
| Working hard | 49 | 54 |
| Generosity | 37 | 47 |
| Creativity | 42 | 41 |

*Bibby,* Canada's Teens, *2001: 16*

Some of the largest gaps included the spread on honesty. Only 62% of males thought honesty was important, as compared to 83% of females. Forgiveness also had a twenty-point spread: 67% of females pegged it as important, whereas only 47% of males thought it was important. Politeness and generosity each showed more than a 10% difference between the sexes, with both values higher for the females.

Within the last few years, the commitment to interpersonal values has plummeted for guys, and they seem to be okay with that. Few other places reveal such a split between the sexes! Is society at large, or are families specifically, teaching (directly or indirectly) our young men that forgiveness, honesty, and politeness are feminine qualities?

# What Does This Mean for Youth Ministry?

## Discuss the Spiritual

The move toward a popularized version of postmodernism holds great opportunities for us. It is much easier, and much more natural, to talk on the spiritual level now, as all ethical choices are considered acts of faith. Spiritual topics are not taboo as they once were. Few people tell us, "Don't talk about religion or politics." One server at a restaurant I frequent found out I was a pastor. She was so interested that she sat down in my booth and started to talk about her belief in angels and prayer.

In some ways, those who are still searching for meaning are more open to discussions of spiritual things than many Christians are. At a small-group class I was taking at the University of Toronto, a woman came up to me, looked in my eye and said, "You have been in touch with the spirit world, haven't you?" I told her, "Yes, I am in touch with the spirit world, and in fact I have the Spirit living in me." She nearly jumped through the roof with excitement. She had found someone who had made contact. I had a coffee with her and told her about the Spirit of God, which lives within every Christian. I told her about the guidance, illumination, and comfort the Spirit gives. She sat in rapt attention, finally exclaiming, "Why don't Christians tell people about this?" In this institution of higher learning where, not too many years before, the stated goal of many an educator was to rid their students of silly superstitions, the spiritual was in the hearts and mouths of the students. Students in the class brought in Tarot cards and spiritual readings from many different sources. In another education class, we sat meditating in a circle, with fire, water, and rocks in the middle.

In years past, some youth workers thought that *not* talking about God in their church meetings would make teens more comfortable coming to them. But teens *want* to talk about God. Do not shy away from looking to Jesus for answers to secular teens' problems. Even praying for our students won't seem out of the ordinary to them. I just spoke to a student who started a prayer club in his school. He asks his friends for prayer requests, and prays for them. He has accumulated quite a list of prayers, as his friends are comfortable giving him requests.

## Keep Methods Fresh and the Message Unchanged

Postmodernism challenges us, too. Once everything is taken as faith, faith loses its uniqueness. A youth pastor friend took a group of churched students up to a retreat sponsored by their denomination. Some of the students in the community went along, and several of them accepted Christ's gift of eternal life. One of these students surprised my friend by telling him of her happiness that she was now part of four religions. She was collecting religious experiences the way people from another generation collected sugar spoons.

As Christian youth workers, we may let culture teach us how to communicate, but we must not let it dictate the actual content of our faith. C.S. Lewis complained that, if you are going to change the major tenets of Christ's teachings, at least be polite enough to give the teaching another name, and not Christ's. Jesus was not just one of many who had a vision of God. Jesus was the only cure for a specific problem: Though he was without sin, he died to take away the sins of the world.

Although our message will not change, we must mould our methods to our culture. We need to work our way out of the old transmissional methods of teaching. As Leonard Sweet says, "Want to create change? Give postmoderns a new experience they haven't had before."[7] In the culture of postmodernism, experience precedes explanation. Rational argument can no longer be the front door to our faith, or we will be answering questions that very few are asking. On the other hand if we allow students to *experience* the living God, they will ask us questions enough afterwards.

I was speaking at an event in a northern camp. A university student told me that he was the only Christian in his dorm. The questions, the jabs, and the mocking were building up doubt in his mind, and he was ready to "chuck" his faith. I told him that, as Christians, we do not have absolute rational certainty, but we do have reasons to believe. I gave him a small book on the topic, which he devoured in a day. The book gave him reasons to believe that bolstered his experience of Christianity.

I have seen this time and time again. In postmodern times, students do not reject thinking, they just don't start with it. There are so many options out there, the first thing students want to know is whether an experience worked for someone else. Knowing that God "works" for others builds hope that God may "work" for them. This hope leads to a series of steps toward faith. If students experience God, they will give all that they know of themselves over to all that they know of God. Only then do the questions, the fitting of their experience into a mental framework, begin.

In early church history, people held everything in common and food was distributed throughout the community. But this did not go smoothly, and some widows were missing out on food. So the early church set up another form of leadership that served the community. This type of local church leadership became enshrined and a theology was formed around it. Experience preceded theology.

What teens experience, they value. Knowing this, we need to ask ourselves, "What experiences do we offer to those on their way to God?" In Acts, chapter ten, the prayers and actions of those on the path to God got the Gentile Cornelius' attention. What in your youth programs will help teens on their way to God to sense the God's presence? Singing and praying to God are good ways to feel a part of God's community.

## Stay Humble in Your Beliefs

Leave room for uncertainty and mystery in what you teach teenagers. The past generation tried to nail everything down into certainty. Reality is much messier than that; we must remember what C.S. Lewis tried to teach us in the Narnia series: that the Lion we serve is good, but not tame. One part of God's nature is creativity. Just look, for example, at the various ways God led Joshua to win battles: He walked around the walls to conquer one city, laid an ambush for another, asked the sun to stand still for yet another – never the same battle plan twice. Remember how Jesus healed: touching some, making spit mud for others, not even coming into contact with still others. Our God sometimes moves among us; at other times, God seems strangely silent. Those Christians who try and make formulas for how God always moves will eventually disappoint the teens they teach. God cannot be forced to do anything.

Christians often have a naive belief that we can have objective (pure and perfect) knowledge of all that is God's. We can't. We are humans, fallible: "For we know in part and we prophesy in part, but when perfection comes, the imperfect disappears. "(1 Cor 13:9-10) Even with the help of the Scriptures and the Holy Spirit, we do not have perfect clarity on all things. Some things I am much more sure of: for example, that the central message of the Gospel is that God can make His home within individuals, giving them a whole new life. The Bible is clear on this point. Other points of theology, such as the Sovereignty of God and the free will of humans, I would argue for (though perhaps not die for), because as I read the Book of books, one side of the theological argument seems the better of the options. On some of the finer points of Jesus' future return, I have my opinions but I may not argue these, as the Scriptures give us only a glimpse of what is to come.

We do not know everything. Some things remain a mystery, teasing our hearts into the worship of the vastness of who God is and what God is doing. Praise God for His mystery! Our teens will understand this, and will respond to a faith that still requires faith.

## Use Religious Language Carefully

We must be careful in how we use Christian language around our teens. Our vocabulary will likely be foreign to most. They will not understand the words we use or, worse, they will misunderstand the lessons we teach. On the one hand, we need to use words that describe what we do in terms they understand. For example, in my church we have life stories instead of "testimonies," the sermon is a talk, our deacons are a vision team, people who are non-Christians are people on their way to God. On the other hand, our teenagers want to understand the ancient meanings of words that are important to us. For example, asking forgiveness is more than saying you're sorry; it involves the repentance of changing one's mind. To ask for forgiveness means you would not do the same deed again if given the chance.

There are many words we should not strike from our language. Grace, mercy, justice, and reconciliation are loaded concepts that can never be accurately described with a secular word. In instances such as these, we need to work hard to define terms, perhaps with a story, so we can help teens change their culture's value dictionaries.

## Encourage Modelling

Our teenagers of both sexes need to see more male role models. There are currently too few males modelling Christ-like qualities. This void fosters the idea among young males that our values are not for them.

Two things are needed: First, we need to actively recruit leaders from both sexes for our youth group. If you are the only leader in the group, get looking. Second, we need leaders who are willing to model their behaviour openly. All too often, adults grow to see their faith as a private affair and don't vocalize the processes they go through. But how else will a teen learn honesty, if not by observing an honest adult? The same is true of generosity, gentleness, mercy, and forgiveness. These qualities will not grow in teens until they are demonstrated by obvious modelling.

We must also celebrate teen modelling. A young woman in our church, Tina, made the decision to call Christ her own. She understood that she had joined a new community where God, her King, desired holiness. Over the previous few years, she had shoplifted from many stores. As a part of her new life, she went back to each of the stores, apologized for stealing from them, and offered to pay them back. The store managers were dumbfounded. What were they to do? Some wondered if they should call the police; others just wondered why she was doing this. When the bill was added up, she owed over a thousand dollars. The news of this leaked out in our community, and the students came alive. Through grassroots conversations alone, the students raised all the money in a week, and Tina was able to pay back every store. This is what it means to both come face to face with Jesus Christ and His church. Models of values defined by the Scriptures need to be multiplied and celebrated throughout the community of Christ.

Language changes, and so must we. I love the question that Leonard Sweet asks: "Will I live the time God has given me? Or will I live a time I would prefer to have?"[8] The truth of who God is never changes. To understand what that means in this age, and learn how to communicate it, we must be willing to constantly learn and change. If we set concrete in the local church, it will be only as a grave marker.

## To Do Today

- Teach integrity by having students make promises to themselves and keep them. For example, have teens make and keep a promise to get up at a certain time in the morning.
- During every worship service, invite those on their way to God to experience Him by praying and singing to God.
- Schedule a meeting for your leaders to discuss how they are modelling values to the students.
- As a project for a Bible study, make up a Christian dictionary of words.
- Discuss with your youth group the different values of men and women and how they affect relationships.

## CHAPTER ELEVEN
# Images of Youth Work

Y ou may have heard the story of the blind men studying the elephant. Each grabbed separately at the trunk, the tusk, the legs, the ears. Each confidently concluded that they had discovered, respectively, a snake, a spear, a tree, and a fan. In their finite wisdom, none got a true understanding of the elephant, nor could they tell which way it was headed.

As we wrap up this project, we feel much like those blind men. We have confidently given you our view of youth ministry – a beast much more complicated than an elephant. Social analysts have suggested that studying society is like trying to examine an elephant that is going in all directions at once, and losing and gaining appendages as it lumbers along. We just don't have a chance of getting it "right." Still, we had at our disposal a rare and precious data source: teenagers' responses to a survey given early in a new millennium. We then moved from description to prescription as confidently as we could. Yet our prescriptions, if acted on in isolation, could leave gifted youth workers with an unbalanced understanding of youth ministry – or worse yet, lead them to think they need to foist what we do in our situations on their own special teenagers.

Hence, we propose in this chapter to step away from the survey, to give you instead some images and principles that can guide youth ministry in a variety of settings. There were threads of assumptions running through the previous pages that came from our walk with God and years of youth ministry practice. Leaving the statistics and theory aside, we wish to flesh out these assumptions.

A lot of good ink has been spilt at the tail end of the second millennium about the decline of organized religion and a subjective, reactionary, postmodern shift. People of faith have struggled for coherent responses. We in Christian youth work have played a strategic role in attempting to understand and live with integrity in changing times. In an increasingly fragmented and diverse world, we have humbly conceded that formulas don't work. There is no one "right way" to do youth ministry.

Still, we hold out that certain ministry principles bring coherence to youth work. Most are not unique to us – we have borrowed them from wise mentors, and now pass them on to you. The metaphors that follow in this chapter lay a foundation for youth work.

## Youth Workers Are Bridges

I was once driving in western New York beside the Erie Canal. The road took a sudden turn to go up and over the canal. There before me was a one-lane bridge. I couldn't see over to the other side. A yield sign slowed my entry. I honked a couple of times, crept forward and imagined that at any moment a car would come barrelling my way from the other direction. As I got off the bridge on the other side, I noticed another yield sign – this time in my rearview mirror. To avoid a crippling collision, caution was needed in both directions.

As youth workers, we stand as a strategic connection between the two cultures of teens and adults, with one foot comfortably and firmly planted in both worlds. We invite both sides to come across, to understand the other. We advocate slowness and caution, advising those on each side to "beep their horns" as they meet in the middle.

To the adults, we become youth advocates. Adults were once adolescents themselves – a luxury of perspective that teens do not have – yet sometimes youth workers encounter adults with amnesia about the teen years. Tragically, adults all too often believe the "youth are a problem" stereotype. Good youth workers remember adolescence and encourage adults to remember theirs.

One way to remind adults is to engage them in a generalize-personalize exercise. First, ask them to list several qualities of teenagers. Write them on a whiteboard. The list invariably ends up holding pretty nasty stereotypes – qualities such as selfishness, rudeness, and rashness. So far in the exercise, adults will seem to prefer the wine-making approach to adolescence: Seal teenagers into barrels at age thirteen, and take them out again – nicely aged and mellowed – when they turn twenty. Now ask these adults to describe a teenager they know, or their own qualities when they were teenagers. The words you will write on the board now are quite different – "creative, fun-loving, eager to learn."

When we allow negative generalizations to set the agenda for how we treat specific people, we go wrong. Youth workers must take seriously their responsibility to become cheerleaders for youth. If we will not do this, who will? There are so many stories of the good things teens do. We must make sure these stories are shared. Adults in our community can use us to understand and then respect teens as emerging adults growing in responsibility. As adults form relationships with enthusiastic youth advocates, they will be freed from their misunderstandings.

To be meaningful connectors, youth workers also need to be firmly and comfortably rooted in the adult community. If you are not so planted, to put it bluntly – get a life! A small number of youth workers have friendships only with their youth. They may simply be delaying the process of growing up. If you find yourself in this group, ask yourself what you are modelling. There is a reason God does not simply forge relationships with individuals, but rather places them in a community. As youth workers, we need to be part of a local church. There we will find adult connections and be pushed to get along with all age groups, see all the gifts available, and have some real accountability.

On the other side of the bridge, we need to lift up adults for the teenagers. For many youth workers, this is the more difficult side to advocate. We often see the adults as the protectors of outmoded traditions, people who focus on worldly rather than eternal things. Yet many adults do live with their eyes on eternity. We need to find these adults and hold them up as examples. If we do not advocate a positive view of adulthood to our teens, who will?

Part of this role of being bridges between the adult and youth worlds includes creating places where relationships between generations can be built. Without intergenerational connections society suffers. Psychologist and anthropologist Stephen Glenn has documented that in every culture where there is a lack of interaction between generations, an increase in juvenile delinquency occurs.[1] Award-winning poet and translator Robert Bly has observed the increased fracturing of intergenerational connectedness over time.[2] Historically, many people, in coming to the "new world," left behind family connections. The trend widened as our parents left the concept of extended family. In our day, the nuclear family is being shaken up. And in our school systems, children experience age-specific grades. Our culture is not the most fertile ground for interaction between generations. This presents a huge opportunity for Christians to rise up and provide a place for dialogue, interaction, and, yes, friendship between generations!

## Youth Workers Are Spotlights

Have you ever driven around a big city at night and seen one of those large spotlights coursing through the night sky? On occasion, I find myself turning an extra corner, drawn to the origin of the spotlight. Sometimes a grand event is being illuminated, and movie stars are on view. Other times the spotlight simply lights up a used-car lot. As Christian youth workers, we are the light of Jesus that shines in the darkness. Whether we like it or not, if we have built relationships with teenagers, we have given them a light to follow. Remember: Whenever you are with teenagers, you are walking "all lit up," modelling behaviour, attitudes, and interests simply by working with them.

Adolescents have their eyes on the people around them as well as on themselves. Erik Erikson described this as simultaneous observation of others and reflection on what that observation means to the adolescent's identity.[3] On various levels of consciousness, adolescents are piecing together who they want to become. When a significant adult develops a relationship with an adolescent, the adult's life offers options as the adolescent makes choices affecting identity. Various traits may be highlighted in the mind of the teenager: "She is so articulate"; "He has a lot of confidence in front of people"; "She has an awesome amount of sensitivity." The adolescent may pick up from the adult behaviours, values, and perhaps a set of underlying assumptions that Yamamoto describes as "a way of seeing life."[4] As emotional involvement increases, identification takes over from imitation and produces results that persist over time.

You are the light of example to your teenagers. Don't hide your light; allow it to shine strongly in the lives of the teens you are called to work with. Make sure that the light you shine to them is pure, filled with the love of Christ.

A serious question flows from this: Are we illuminating something worthwhile or, when all is finally said and done, will we have been no more than a dazzling disappointment along some teenagers' journey? If this question haunts you, there is hope. Freedom comes from truth-telling. Spend time in honest dialogue with God and trusted friends, and put things right. Our teens need people of integrity and spiritual maturity in their lives.

Following are some principles, borrowed from Lawrence Kohlberg's work, for enhancing your modelling.[5]

First, treat teens as equals while being wholly your self.[6] Adolescents do not want to be controlled by anyone. Adults who have an air of being in charge will doom relationships with teens from the start. Adults are often seen to behave one way with their peers and another with adolescents. Adolescents consider this behaviour two-faced; it announces that they are being treated not as equals but as children.

Second, spend time at the task of modelling. As a drug lord in downtown Manhattan said, this is a war and whoever spends the most time wins. Adults should be a part of the physical world of adolescents. Relationships with adults need to build memories, so attend events and spend unhurried time together. If we spend time with teens only in the context of church programs, they will feel as if they are just part of our job and not true friends. Many adult volunteers play miniature golf, ride go-carts, bowl, play video games, skate, toboggan, or go to an amusement park with their teens. Everyday activities like washing cars, baking brownies, or shopping can be added to the list. In fact, many adults find simply going about the day's activities – while modelling everyday reactions to life – the best way to spend time with teens. Alongside these activities, our adult leaders participate in the more serious activities of prayer and Bible study, modelling how the spiritual can belong with the everyday.

Third, give positive, honest feedback. Adults act as the audience for adolescents, giving feedback in various ways. Adolescents continually monitor this feedback. Recently, a teen mentioned to a mutual friend that, when talking in a group setting, I didn't call her by name. She believed I must hate her, simply because I had forgotten her name, one of the hundreds I had learned that night. I was significant to her, and she was looking for approval. Adult volunteers must remember names, smile, and acknowledge an adolescent's presence to communicate social approval.

We often suggest to adult volunteers that they guard their humour, particularly the kind that is at the expense of the adolescent. Adults need to be aware that every reaction is amplified in the adolescent's mind and be sure not to give unintentionally hurtful feedback. Whether we like it or not, we provide a mirror for teens and they look hard at how they are being perceived.

Fourth, build similarities. Teens are more likely to model themselves after you if you are competent in some area, or if you demonstrate similarities to them. We must be students of ourselves. "What am I good at?" "What can I improve?" "What competencies can I pass on to the next generation?" Then model your strengths. For example, if you are a great organizer, model that to the teens you work with.

Common interests build relationships. The Dale Carnegie course on "how to win friends and influence people" trains individuals to develop common interests with those around them. This course taps into wisdom concerning relevance. If you have similar interests to mine, then we have something to talk about that "interests" both of us. Your interests are relevant to my life. This makes it easier for a relationship to be born between us.

A young college student asked me to mentor him. After some time, I discovered that he wanted to work in an international setting, and knew that I had some international experience. Once I knew this fact, I understood that I should enhance this aspect of our common interests. I set up various lunches with people who worked internationally, during and after which we had great discussions. The similarities between us and the relevance that brought to my mentorship deepened our relationship and the modelling process.

Fifth, risk being vulnerable – the more you share of yourself, the more the teens will model after you. Adults who can be vulnerable are often met with growing openness on the part of teenagers. As the levels of sharing and communication are deepened, a growing attachment builds in the relationship, and the level of modelling deepens as well.

In issues of vulnerability, adults often feel that they are there for the adolescents' problems, and should not share their own struggles. To a degree this may be true, in that the goal is to help adolescents in identity formation. However, unless there is some degree of reciprocity, adolescents will not develop much attachment or respect, nor will they grow sufficiently through the modelling experience. How can adolescents see how I handle conflict unless I let them see some of the real conflict in my life?

Sharing vulnerability does not have to mean sharing negative life experiences. You can show vulnerability by sharing what you have learned while reading a favourite book, or what you loved about a movie. The important thing is to allow adolescents to enter your world.

## Youth Workers Are Time-Braiders

When my daughter was younger, she wanted to braid the hair of her Barbie. She wound two strands around each other and sat back and watched as they unwound easily. No matter how hard she tried, she couldn't get the two to stay together. A braid of three strands, however, stays tightly wound. In youth ministry, we need to braid together three aspects: work with individuals, work with groups, and work with tasks.

Have you noticed how many youth workers become unravelled? One of the reasons is lack of balance. A youth worker was not accepted by his teens, and his group meetings were not going well. To compensate, he spent all his time building a youth café with television sets and matching awnings and tablecloths. The church asked him to leave because he spent too much time on this task. Tasks are important, but they need to be balanced with individual and group work.

Another youth worker ran a drop-in ministry. He was great at individual relationships. When he walked through the downtown core, teens called out his name in recognition. However, after some time he became discouraged. The teens were friendly and interested in a relationship with Jesus, but few of them were making moves spiritually. He had not allowed the power of God to work through a group. Individual relationships are central to youth work, but without a group we lack the power of community.

Alternatively, we have all come across pastors who are so interested in building their group that individuals suffer. Teens may move in to a group because they are won by the fun, but they will find the place hollow if no time is spent building relationships. By the time high-school graduation comes, they may have "graduated" from spiritual beliefs as well, because they never made their faith personal.

Balance is crucial. I remember my first youth pastorate. The church leaders wanted me in the office working on tasks for three hours a day. I was upset. I thought, "What can a youth pastor do in an office? We are to be out meeting students, building relationships." Do I ever kick myself now, thinking of the ministry I could have accomplished by taking some time for tasks. Tasks may include making phone calls, writing letters or e-mails, designing advertisements, reading, working on the physical space, or thinking over missions, roles, and goals.

Many youth workers are relational, and because this is central to youth it is a great start. However, great leaders also seek to develop in areas where they are not as strong. I am not a goal-oriented person, yet I take at least five days a year to get away from all people and set goals. Under the guidance of prayer, I have discovered various roles God wants me to play in this short life of mine. For example, I believe God wants me to be an expert in the spiritual realm, a great husband and father, a visionary leader at my church. Since I only have one life to live I want to be a master at every level. While on my retreats, I pray through each of my roles, asking God to guide me in what He wants to do this next year. After some time of refining, I set up goals. In my role as an excellent husband, I set these goals: To go for a daily walk with my wife and to take three weekend getaways with her. I then write them in my schedule book. To me this is heavy-duty goal setting. It works against my spontaneous nature, but because of it I have a better relationship with my wife than I would have otherwise. I must cut away time to perform tasks – goal-oriented time – or my relationships suffer. If you are always surrounded by other people, eventually your use to them will become diminished.

Most of us understand the beauty of relationships. However, for task-oriented individuals who read the last paragraph and cheered loudly, this anecdote is for you. Robin is in charge of setting up the sound and music equipment for our church. This task requires a team of five people working for two hours. We don't have a building of our own, so we meet in the theatre of a local college. Robin is a very task-oriented person. In the past, he only wanted to get the job done; if his crew members had personal problems, they just needed to "suck it up." But in the last few years Robin has wanted to grow in leadership, so he did what was hardest for him – he started to ask how his crew was doing. He spent time building relationships with his team. They now stand in a circle before they unload even one item, find out where everybody is at in their lives, and pray for each other. It puts a smile on my face when I see this group of big guys, all dressed to lift heavy equipment, talking about their lives and caring for each other out in a parking lot. If we add a relational level to everything we do in youth ministry, depth will follow.

There is a movement within some Christian circles against having any kind of youth group. These people have seen the ineffectiveness (some assumed, some true) of giant programming and are opting for one-on-one experiences. This may be good for those students who are ready for this, but some things can be learned only in a group setting. Even Jesus did very little one-on-one ministry. He took his twelve, or at least his three, with him. He even went in for big events, such as the feeding of the five thousand. And perhaps 150 disciples followed him through much of his ministry. Now that's a big group. The very concept of the church assumes that some things can be done in a large group that cannot be done in a much smaller one. A large enough group is needed so that various people's spiritual gifts will have a niche and an outlet. Outreach to the community around you also requires a larger group.

Teens will not be drawn to you as a leader unless they feel the pull of a new tribe. Too many drop-in ministry workers do not have a Christian tribe forming somewhere in their ministry; instead, the ministry's only pull is in individual relationships. As a result, very secular teens come in and go out unchanged and unchallenged to go the next step in their spiritual walk.

We need to help our teens to stand strong as individuals, but we work against the nature of teens if we don't also provide for them a group of positive peer pressure. Part of our job as youth workers is to build a tribe apart – a place where the values and presence of Jesus are celebrated. When I meet with youth workers and they tell me of their work with individuals, I ask them to follow up on that work by creating a group for their students to be a part of. The group itself is a ministry tool. Teenagers will be won by a group with positive and healthy values. These values do not happen by accident. It takes work to build up a group image students can be a part of, to build a place where God's love rules – a place to which students will happily invite their friends. A name needs to be chosen, an atmosphere developed, acts of internal love intentionally performed. The old days of teens inviting their friends to "youth group" in a smelly church basement are long gone.

We hope we have persuaded you about the importance of balance. Youth workers must ask God for an understanding of their natural strengths in ministry – whether in individual work, group work, or the performance of tasks – and under God's guidance, weave in the missing strands.

## Youth Workers Are Wildlife Reserve Officers

There are wildlife reserves around the world in which animals are kept safe from the encroachment of humans. In one of my favourite wildlife shows, a reserve officer, taking his life in his hands, sets a trapped crocodile free. Gingerly he sidesteps the croc's thrashing and opens the trap. The huge animal swims free as, with a smile, the officer whispers, "There ya go, little fellow." That man had respect and awe for what such an animal could do, and his job was to give it the space and freedom it needed.

We need to model ourselves after this reserve officer in how we treat our teens. Teenagers possess great leadership ability that can have a massive impact on our society. Seldom do people have more friends than during their teenage years. Those in college have close friends, but in smaller circles. Adults have even smaller circles of friends. Teens are at a point when they are searching for who they want to be. We must never manipulate, but neither can we be silent. In the great marketplace of ideas, faiths, and values, the voice of Christ must be heard at its strongest during this time of life. For it is now that identities are looking for a form to take. These emerging adults can have a life-altering experience with God, and bring a group of friends along for the ride.

We know of high-school students who have led many of their friends to faith in Christ. Some of those friends now serve God in ministries of their own. The ripples of influence go on.

We know of a youth group that wrote and performed their own Easter musical. The performance was taped by a television station, which has been running the show every year at Easter. The ripples of influence go on.

The challenge is to avoid underselling our youth. They are champing at the bit to make a difference in the world, yet we sometimes offer them only pizza and "four on the couch" in the church basement on Friday night. Often, teen ministry is nothing more than entertainment or babysitting. It is not enough merely to "keep the kids off the streets." Students are capable of much more. The millennials are not lying back in apathy – they are fired up and ready to go. Act boldly in encouraging student leadership. Raise the bar for your students; challenge those who will rise to the call.

While writing this page I received an e-mail from a student who is losing sleep over how to get the great news of Jesus Christ out to his friends. This is the time. Teens have the contacts, they are searching for meaning, and they have the ability to do great things. As we fulfill our role as wildlife reserve officers, teaching students how to survive on their own and giving them the power to do so, our burden is lessened. Teens are remarkable creatures, indeed, so set them free to change the world!

## Youth Workers Are Bricklayers

Before laying a brick, a bricklayer stands back and evaluates how many bricks are needed for the different layers and, given the climate of the area and the purpose of the wall, what kind of cement to mix. Youth ministry has various distinct layers – some social action, some evangelism, some growth in the spiritual disciplines, and perhaps some leadership training. In the last twenty years, a move has been afoot to understand how we can stack our programs and cement each layer better.[7] Some see youth ministry as a funnel: outreach events funnel down into growth events, which funnel down into leadership training events. Others use the picture of a layer cake, where the bottom layer represents the fun seekers, the middle layer represents those fewer students who are willing to come and grow, and the top layer represents the few who are willing to come and minister as servant leaders.

We do many things in our youth groups without asking who the target audience is. Are we holding this event for those on their way to God? Are we holding this event for those already convinced? Many small youth groups have never gone through this process of evaluation. Make a list of what you do with your group and the purpose of each event. If you are like many groups, most of the time you spend with youth is for Christian fellowship or Christian growth. You are limiting your growth by not having any meetings designed for those who are still *on their way* to knowing God personally. Some groups make no time for leadership training, then wonder why their students do not take more initiative. If we don't build a layer of leadership training, our groups will foster fewer leaders.

A good bricklayer makes layers of bricks, rather than laying them all out in one row. In the same way, good youth workers layer their meetings for different purposes. One country church has decided to have one games night a month to reach out into the community, two small-group Bible study nights a month, and one planning meeting with the student leaders. Now a small group has asked what they are doing and why. Another youth group spends one night a week giving social assistance to the area's poor, goes on a yearly evangelistic retreat, and holds a Sunday school class for growing Christians. They decided what they wanted to accomplish, and designed their meetings around their purposes.

Good bricklayers also need to ask what holds each layer together. As youth workers, how do we draw teens from a games night to a Bible study? One church has their small-group leaders attend the weekly outreach concert. The students from the community come for the music and friends, meet the group leaders and are drawn into the small groups by the relationships they form with the leaders. Many ministries forget to think about the cement between the layers. They need to ask what holds the various levels of ministry together. What is the draw from one level to the next?

## Youth Workers Are Seed-Planters

Your youth ministry efforts – though they may seem small – are sure to grow! The miracle is in the seed, not in the farmer, though the farmer may till and water. Here is the beautiful part about youth ministry: With the right perspective, you cannot fail. As Mike Yaconelli said, "The things we do are better than if we were not there." Youth ministry is reaching out to a teen, a teen's parent, another youth worker, with the love of God. No hoopla is necessary. Your activities may be simple, humble, small and ordinary – even, you may think, insignificant. You and God and the person being touched will know you are making a difference, and that is all that really matters.

A godly minister who has worked with troubled youth in our area for more than two decades takes a ghetto blaster to street people and plays the same worship tape over and over – and people respond! He does not need the expensive sound system or light show that some ministries rely on. This same man, when asked to talk about what he does, simply says, "Some things are meant to be walked in, not publicized."

Do the best you can with what God has given you. No ministry we do is less significant than any other. God's love, not the program, is the power here. Transcendent love takes a wide variety of forms and always – always – leaves its mark. We know of ministries in settings where words cannot be used to share the good news of Jesus. Public schools, for example, book Christian camp facilities for outdoor education classes in which it is inappropriate to discuss religion. Yet as we love unconditionally in these settings, people are drawn to the source of that love. Love softens them, and in time they find Jesus, make him their own master, and give their lives to loving kids the same way they were loved.

Remember that we are God's co-labourers (1 Cor 3:5-9). Depend on God! Any act of love we extend in the name and power of Christ will grow, because God faithfully gardens and waters the seeds we plant.

## Just Be Yourself

We have given you suggestions from the data and our experience. Our recommendations may work in your situation, or they may not. Do not wear them like a burden, or burden others with them, if they do not fit. Be yourself, and find your own call. In his classic essay "In the Name of Jesus," Henri Nouwen challenges Christians to avoid giving into the temptations Jesus faced in the desert, and not be seduced by the enemy of our souls into being relevant, spectacular, or powerful.[8] Instead, be that special person God gifted you to be.

Yes, sociology, education, and other disciplines are helpful to youth ministry. It is important to know youth cultural and developmental patterns, but we must let God's love drive us, not the latest statistics and theories. Rejoice in the ministry of whatever motley crew God surrounds you with! Follow God, and love the people in your community. Help your group be all it can be – and not necessarily a carbon copy of somebody else's group.

As the *Message Bible* puts John 4:23-24:

It is who you are and the way you live that counts before God. Your worship must engage your spirit in the pursuit of truth. That's the kind of people the Father is out looking for – those who are simply and honestly themselves before him in their worship. God is sheer being himself – Spirit. Those who worship him must do it out of their very being, their spirits, their true selves in adoration.

Remember that you and your community are blessed and favoured simply because of Jesus' work on the cross. Our hurting world craves the love you and your youth know and can offer.

Thank you for staying with us during our journey to develop understanding and love for the teenagers of our time. We hope God has been able to speak through our meagre words. The next generation needs to hear of the great deeds of our God, that they may know God personally. Our hearts echo the psalmist who wrote: "Even when I am old and gray, do not forsake me, O God, till I declare your power to the next generation, your might to all who are to come." (Ps 71:18)

# Endnotes

## Introduction

1   Discussions with Jewish, Muslim, Catholic, Mainline Protestant, and Evangelical leaders, Vancouver, British Columbia, November 3–4, 2001, conducted by Reginald Bibby.

2   See, for example, Michael Adams, *Better Happy Than Rich? Canadians, Money and the Meaning of Life* (Toronto: Penguin Books of Canada, 2000), 24–28. Adams highlights Canada's postmodern shift relative to the U.S. with the following statistic: In 1996 a comparative survey found that more than twice as many Americans (44%) than Canadians (20%) agreed with the statement: "Father must be master in his own home." (In 1983, when this variable was first measured, 42% of Canadians agreed!)

3   Donald C. Posterski, *Friendship: A Window on Ministry to Youth* (Scarborough, ON: Project Teen Canada, 1985), xiii.

## CHAPTER ONE The Millennials

1   Generational divisions are an inaccurate science. Some people place the brackets around the millennials a couple of years on either side of the eighties.

2   Neil Howe and William Strauss, *Millennials Rising: The Next Great Generation* (New York: Vintage Books, 2000), 4.

3   Ibid.

4   One cautionary note: The correlation between religious youth-group attendance and positive faith doesn't necessarily demonstrate that youth-group attendance *causes* this growth; some groups may simply be screening out irreligious teens in order to look more spiritual. We advocate that religious youth groups be open for *all youth* to explore at their own level.

5   Rolf Eduard Helmut Muuss, Eli Velder, and Harriet Porton, *Theories of Adolescence* (New York: Random House, 1975), 4.

6   James E. Côté and Anton L. Allahar, *Generation on Hold: Coming of Age in the Late Twentieth Century* (Toronto: Stoddart, 1994).

7   Lethbridge Collegiate Institute, *Kids Will Be Kids*. Used with permission.

8    Stanley Hauwerwaus and William H. Willimon, *Resident Aliens: Life in the Christian Colony* (Nashville: Abingdon Press, 1989), 12.

## CHAPTER TWO Friendship Tribes and Lego Connections

1    Don Posterski, *Friendship: A Window on Ministry to Youth* (Scarborough, ON, Project Teen Canada, 1985), 7.

2    Some psychologists have suggested that females have a stronger relational bent than males. See, for example, Robert Stoller, "A Contribution to the Study of Gender Identity," *International Journal of Psycho-Analysis* 45 (1964): 220–226 (quoted in Carol Gilligan, *In a Different Voice: Psychological Theory and Women's Development* (Cambridge, MA: Harvard University Press, 1993), 7); Nancy J. Chodorow, *The Reproduction of Mothering: Psychoanalysis and the Sociology of Gender* (Berkeley, CA: University of California Press, 1978), 167.

3    Gore Vidal, in Jane Kroger, *Identity in Adolescence: The Balance Between Self and Other* (New York: Routledge, 1988), 1.

4    Patricia Hersch, *A Tribe Apart: A Journey into the Heart of American Adolescence* (New York: Ballantine Books, 1998), 19.

5    Dawson McAllister with Pat Springle, *Saving the Millennial Generation: New Ways to Reach the Kids You Care About in These Uncertain Times* (Nashville: Thomas Nelson, 1999), 85.

6    Malcolm Gladwell, *The Tipping Point: How Little Things Can Make a Big Difference* (Boston: Little Brown, 2000), 30–58.

7    Howard Gardner, *Multiple Intelligences: The Theory in Practice* (New York: Basic Books, 1993), 22–25.

8    Lawrence Richards, *Youth Ministry* (Grand Rapids, MI: Zondervan, 1972), 123.

9    Laurent A. Daolz, *Mentor: Guiding the Journey of Adult Learners* (San Francisco: Jossey Bass, 1999), 225.

## CHAPTER THREE Weightless Authority

1    Leonard I. Sweet, *Postmodern Pilgrims: First Century Passion for the 21st Century Church* (Nashville: Broadman and Holman, 2000), 27.

2    Robert Dahl, "The Concept of Power," *Behavioral Science* 2, no. 3 (July 1957): 203–4.

3    Jeffrey C. Isaac, "Beyond the Three Faces of Power: A Realist Critique." In *Rethinking Power*, edited by Thomas E. Wartenburg (New York: State University of New York Press, 1992), 43.

4    Jurgen Habermas, "Hannah Arendt: On the Concept of Power." In *Philosophical-Political Profiles*, translated by Fredrick G. Lawrence (Cambridge, MA: M.I.T. Press, 1983), 173; Jeffrey C. Isaac, "After Empiricism: The Realist Alternative." In *Idioms of Inquiry*, edited by Terence Ball (Albany, NY: State University of New York Press, 1987).

5    Terence Ball, "New Faces of Power." In *Rethinking Power*, edited by Thomas E. Wartenburg (New York: State University of New York Press, 1992), 26.

6   Jean Piaget, *Six Psychological Studies* (New York: Vintage Books, 1968), 62.

7   The concept of abuse as an act of high treason comes from personal discussions with and public lectures by New Testament scholar Dr. Rikk Watts, Regent College, University of British Columbia, Vancouver.

8   John French and Bertram Raven, "The Bases of Social Power." In Darwin Cartwright and Alvin Zander, *Group Dynamics* (New York: Harper and Row, 1968).

9   Nicholas Burbules, *Dialogue in Teaching: Theory and Practice* (New York: Teachers College Press, 1993), 36.

## CHAPTER FOUR Cocoon-Ripping Freedom

1   Since adolescence is understood as the transitional time between childhood dependencies and adult responsibilities, the college years, before adult responsibilities are taken up, are seen by many as a time of extended adolescence.

2   College-age adolescents are perhaps the most difficult age group to program for. They have broken free from most things, even programs. Now, for the first time, they are free to go where they like and return home whenever they want to, without parental restraints. One strategy that works in my church is the after-meeting "hangout" time, when the students are free to leave at any time.

3   Psychologist Peter Blos understands adolescence as a process of second individuation: We understand that we are separate human beings at around the age of two and experience a sense of independence; during adolescence, we discover we are separate from our parents, which creates a second wave of independence. Peter Blos, *The Adolescent Passage: Developmental Issues* (New York: International Universities Press, 1979).

4   Erik H. Erikson, Identity: *Youth and Crisis* (New York: W.W. Norton & Company, 1968), 247.

5   Josh McDowell, *The Disconnected Generation* (Nashville: Word Publ., 2000), 28.

6   Mary Pipher, *Reviving Ophelia: Saving the Selves of Adolescent Girls* (New York: Ballantine Books, 1994).

7   The median age at first marriage of women in 1960 was twenty years old; in 1991 it was twenty-four. U.S. Bureau of the Census, reported in Neil Howe and William Strauss, *13th Gen: Abort, Retry, Ignore, Fail?* (New York: Vintage, 1993), 156.

8   A 1992 MTV survey of 1,000 young adults aged eighteen to twenty-nine found that they considered a lack of jobs or economic opportunities to be the single greatest obstacle facing their generation. American job growth was 27% over the 1970s and a projected 13% over the 1990s. Under the heading "McJobs and Temps," Geoffrey Holtz writes, "While the economy did add 21 million new jobs during the eighties, these were overwhelmingly concentrated in

the service industry." Geoffrey T. Holtz, *Welcome to the Jungle: The Why Behind "Generation X"* (New York: St. Martin's Press, 1995), 143–51.

9    David Elkind, *All Grown Up and No Place to Go: Teenagers in Crisis* (Reading, MA: Addison-Wesley Publishing, 1971), 93–114.

10   Robert Bly has written two books on this topic: *The Sibling Society* (Reading, MA: Addison-Wesley Longman, 1996) and *Where Have All the Parents Gone?* (New York: Sound Horizons, 1996).

11   Richard J. Foster, *Freedom of Simplicity: Finding Harmony in a Complex World* (New York: Harper, 1981), 114.

12   Stephen Glenn observed that, in North American before the Second World War, approximately 70% of people lived in rural areas where large families were empowered with significant work. After the Second World War, the percentage shifted so that 70% of people lived in urban centres, where the number of chores was smaller. Glenn believes this shift is one of the cultural causes of adolescence. Stephen Glenn, "Building Capable Students," General Session, taped at the National Youth Workers' Convention in Chicago, Illinois (El Cajon, CA: Youth Specialties, 1988).

Erik Erikson saw three catalysts to identity formation in adolescents: the natural, biological unfolding (puberty and cognitive changes); personal history (family life); and the larger historical context. Urbanization can certainly be seen as a larger historical context.

The disappearance of significant work and the resulting feelings of powerlessness can be seen in other countries, where urbanization and modernization are taking place, as well. In 1997, Nowa, the General Secretary for the Kenya Students Christian Fellowship, travelled to North America to study the culture of North American teens. Nowa had been working with Kenyan teenagers for fifteen years in rural areas, and he observed a distinct teen culture in the urban centres of Kenya that was very similar to North American adolescent culture. According to Nowa, the move from the farm to the city made "North Americans" out of Kenyan adolescents. (Nowa, conversation with Dave Overholt, Hamilton, Ontario, May 1997).

13   Henri J.M. Nouwen, *The Return of the Prodigal Son: A Story of Homecoming* (New York: Image Books [Doubleday], 1994), 122–123.

14   C.S. Lewis, *Mere Christianity* (San Francisco: HarperCollins, 1952), 50.

15   Douglas Coupland, *Life After God* (New York: Pocket Books, 1994), 359.

16   Frank Smith, *The Book of Learning and Forgetting* (New York: Teachers College Press, 1998), 3–5, 10.

## CHAPTER FIVE Marinated in Music and Media

1    The hours per day that these activities entail were estimated as follows: attending school, 5; listening to music, 3; watching movies, 2; reading, 2; jamming/working on music, 2; attending concerts/raves, 4; attending religious services, 1.5. Watching television was calculated at 2.71 hours daily, and work time was varied in keeping with PTC 2000 findings. The numbers of days per

year that teens engaged in these activities was multiplied by the estimated hours per day to determine the annual hours. To further examine the method and rationale for this approximate – but insightful – calculation, consult James A. Penner, "Adolescent Religious Disposition in Canada: An Exploratory Analysis" (master's thesis: University of Lethbridge, 1995), 97, 98.

2    Mary Pipher, *Reviving Ophelia: Saving the Selves of Adolescent Girls* (New York: Ballantine Books, 1994), 57.

3    Ibid.

4    Steven Crites, "The Narrative Quality of Experience," *The Journal of the American Academy of Religion* 39 (September 1971): 303.

5    Douglas Rushkoff, *Playing the Future: What We Can Learn from Digital Kids* (New York: Riverhead, 1999).

6    Rikk Watts, conversation with James Penner, Regent College, University of British Columbia, Vancouver, 12 March 2001.

## CHAPTER SIX  Digital Divides

1    Douglas Rushkoff, *Playing the Future: What We Can Learn from Digital Kids* (New York: Riverhead, 1999), 5.

2    Don Tapscott, *Growing up Digital: The Rise of the Net Generation* (New York: McGraw-Hill, 1998), 48–50.

3    Clifford Stoll, *Silicon Snake Oil: Second Thoughts on the Information Highway* (New York: Anchor Books, 1995), 43.

4    Keith Knight, "Putting Computer Technology in Its Place," *Christian Week* (17 April 2001), 6.

5    Jeff Carter, "Virtual Community and the Millennial Generation: An Investigation of Authentic Qualities of Community via the Internet for Canadian Christian Youth" (D.Min. thesis: McMaster Divinity College, Hamilton, Ontario, 2001).

6    Leonard Sweet, *Soul Tsunami* (Grand Rapids, MI: Zondervan. 1999), 219.

7    Reginald W. Bibby, *Canada's Teens: Today, Yesterday, and Tomorrow* (Toronto: Stoddart, 2001), 62.

8    The Alpha video course features Church of England Rector Nicky Gumble of Holy Trinity Brampton Church in London, England. For more information check out www.alpha.org.

9    Quinten Schultze, "Faith and Cyberspace," course lecture at Regent College, Vancouver, British Columbia, summer 1998.

10   Bibby, *Canada's Teens*, 47.

## CHAPTER SEVEN  Dancing with Consumerism

1    Doug Stewart, "Hit Music Video Sheds Light on a Report on Canadian Teen Lifestyles," *Youth Marketing Report* (6 August 2001).

2    Jancee Dunn, "The Secret Life of Teenage Girls," *Rolling Stone* (11 November 1999), 107.

3   Anne Sutherland and Beth Thompson, *Kidfluence: Why Kids Today Mean Business* (Toronto: McGraw-Hill, 2001), 95.

4   Catherine Fairley, "Boom," *Toronto Star,* 22 June 2001, p. D1.

5   Sutherland & Thompson, *Kidfluence,* 106.

6   Ibid., 101.

7   Dunn, "Secret Life," 107.

8   Fairley, "Boom," p. D1.

9   Dunn, "Secret Life," 114.

10  Of historical note is the high level of anxiety at the individual and macro levels in 1992. This was a recessionary period at the tail end of the Mulroney years in Canada when government spending was perceived to be recklessly pushing up the national debt, businesses were restructuring, and youth employment was high. (The 1990s economic downturn also correlated to a more general pessimism among youth about other social issues. See Reginald W. Bibby and Donald C. Posterski, "Young People See Problems Everywhere," *Teen Trends* (Toronto: Stoddart, 1992), 73.

11  Dunn, "Secret Life," 112.

12  Ibid., 116.

13  Naomi Klein, *No Logo: Taking Aim at the Brand Bullies* (Toronto: Knopf Canada, 2000), 21.

14  Joel Swerdlow, "Global Culture," *National Geographic* (August 1999), 17.

15  Klein, *No Logo,* 21.

16  Ibid., 19.

17  Jean Kilbourne, *Deadly Persuasion: Why Women and Girls Must Fight the Addictive Power of Advertising* (New York: The Free Press, 1999), 85.

18  See Benjamin R. Barber, *Jihad vs McWorld: How Globalism and Tribalism Are Reshaping the World* (New York: McGraw-Hill, 1998) for examples of how celebrities, products, and communication lines are merging in the present global capitalistic system.

19  Joan Uhelszki, "Britney chooses Pepsi," *Rolling Stone* (8 February 2001).

20  Dunn, "Secret Life," 109.

21  Kilbourne, *Deadly Persuasion,* 44.

22  John Wesley, *The Journal of John Wesley,* ed. Percy Livingstone Parker (Chicago: Moody, 1951), 409.

23  Kilbourne, *Deadly Persuasion,* 68.

24  Ibid., 67–68.

25  Report of the Club of Rome, *The Limits of Growth,* as quoted by Richard J. Foster, *Freedom of Simplicity: Finding Harmony in a Complex World* (New York: Harper, 1981), 224.

26  George Gerbner, "Television Violence: The Art of Asking the Wrong Question," quoted in Kilbourne, *Deadly Persuasion,* 56.

27  Tom Beaudoin, "Three's Company," *US Catholic Journal* (September 2000), 11.

28    The phrase "back in the box" and the idea of using a game to illustrate the emptiness of life was taken from John Ortberg, from Willow Creek Community Church in South Barrington, Illinois.

29    Dale Lang, address to a Maple Ridge, British Columbia, high-school assembly, 20 February 2001.

## CHAPTER EIGHT Mind Grinders

1    Reginald W. Bibby and Donald C. Posterski, *Teen Trends* (Toronto: Stoddard, 1992), 73.

2    Patricia Hersch, *A Tribe Apart: A Journey into the Heart of American Adolescence* (New York: Ballantine Books, 1998), 33.

3    Stephen Glenn, "Building Capable Students," General Session, taped at the National Youth Workers' Convention in Chicago, Illinois (El Cajon, CA: Youth Specialists, 1988).

4    Ibid.

5    Hersch, *A Tribe Apart*, 68.

6    Rev. Dale Lang, address to a Maple Ridge, British Columbia, high-school assembly, 20 February 2001.

7    Hersch, *A Tribe Apart*, 64.

8    Jean Piaget, *Six Psychological Studies* (New York: Vintage Books, 1968), 63.

9    Erik Erikson, *Identity, Youth and Crisis* (New York: W.W. Norton & Company, 1968), 22–23.

10    Gordon MacDonald, *Ordering Your Private World* (Nashville: Oliver Nelson, 1984), 80.

11    Richard A. Swenson, M.D., *The Overload Syndrome: Learning to Live Within Your Limits* (Colorado Springs: Navpress, 1998), 68–72.

12    *Reasons to Believe: signposts for those on the journey to God* is a teen-friendly resource that can be helpful in answering teens' bigger questions. This book can be ordered from Church on the Rock: www.churchontherock.on.ca.

## CHAPTER NINE Romancing Risk

1    Lynn E. Ponton, *The Romance of Risk: Why Teenagers Do the Things They Do* (New York: Basic Books, 1997), 2.

2    David Elkind, *All Grown Up and No Place to Go* (Reading, MA: Addison-Wesley Publishing, 1971), 36–38.

3    Ponton, *The Romance of Risk*, 8.

4    Ibid., 20.

5    Ibid., 30.

6    Reginald W. Bibby, *Project Canada Consultation on Research and Ministry (PCCRM)*, (2–4 November 2001), 20

7    Rikk Watts, conversation with James Penner, Regent College, University of British Columbia, Vancouver, 12 March 2001.

8    Bibby, *PCCRM* (2–4 November 2001), 11.

## CHAPTER TEN The New Dictionary of Values

1. Reginald W. Bibby, *Project Canada Consultation on Research and Ministry (PCCRM)* (2–4 November 2001), 20.

2. Ibid., 10.

3. It is beyond the scope of this book to examine the roots of the personalization of truth from existentialism through modernism to postmodernism. It is enough to understand the waters in which our teens are swimming. Also there are two different worlds of reality in philosophy: the scholarly world, in which philosophical systems are argued in their theoretical and academic contexts; and the world at large, in which a philosophy is popularized and applied. Since we are attempting to understand the lack of ethical foundations as a perceived reality of teens, we will not be looking at philosophy in an academic way.

4. J. Richard Middleton and Brian Walsh, *Truth Is Stranger Than It Used to Be: Biblical Faith in a Postmodern Age* (Downer's Grove, IL: Intervarsity Press, 1995), 31.

5. The following is a synopsis of postmodernism by Jason Shriner: "The nineteenth century unleashed numerous attacks on the empiricist agenda from many angles. Not meaning to discount important figures such as Nietzsche, Hegel or Kierkegaard, the cracking of the empiricist foundation can easily be seen through the recognition of the anthropological methodology of observer participation (where the notion of a neutral and objective observer was overturned as it became evident that the observer participates in that which s/he observes – i.e., all realities are participated 'in' and cannot be viewed from 'outside of.') The second crack comes with what can loosely be called the linguistic turn in philosophy, where truth and meaning no longer were considered as entities or realities 'out there' but rather as constructs of language – and more specific, the language of user communities. The twentieth century brought this agenda to new heights in which the two battling philosophical systems waged war with each other while society in general enjoyed relative peace moving along on the wave of modernistic technological triumph. What can now be seen as the societal effects of the introduction of 'postmodern' philosophies is the hyperbolic stretch of observer participation to relativism to hyper-individualism (where values become grounded only in the self) and the advancement of the linguistic understanding of truth to the deconstruction of language such that words become powerless to signify anything with certainty." Jason Shriner, personal letter to Dave Overholt, September 2001.

6. Peter A. Angeles, *Harper Collins Dictionary of Philosophy* (Toronto: HarperCollins, 1992), 326.

7. Leonard I. Sweet, *Postmodern Pilgrims: First Century Passion for the 21st Century* (Nashville: Broadman and Holman, 2000), 43.

8. Ibid., 47.

## CHAPTER ELEVEN Images of Youth Work

1   Stephen Glenn, "Building Capable Students," General Session, taped at the National Youth Worker's Convention in Chicago, IL (El Cajon CA: Youth Specialties, 1988).
2   Robert Bly, *Where Have All the Parents Gone?* (New York: Sound Horizons, 1996).
3   Erik Erikson, *Identity: Youth and Crisis* (New York: W.W. Norton & Company, 1968), 22–23.
4   Kaoru Yamamoto, "To See Life Grow: The Meaning of Mentorship," *Theory into Practice* 27, no. 3 (1988), 184.
5   Lawrence Kohlberg, *The Psychology of Moral Development: The Nature and Validity of Moral Stages* (San Francisco: Harper and Row, 1984), 125–53.
6   Natalie S. Eldridge, "Mentoring from a Self-In-Relation Perspective," *Annual Convention of the American Psychological Association* (1990), 4, describes the concept of being wholly oneself with another person.
7   Dann Spader initiated a ministry called Son Life that gives seminars on this concept. Larry Richards before him wrote about such levels of ministry: Lawrence Richards, *Youth Ministry* (Grand Rapids, MI: Zondervan, 1972).
8   Henri Nouwen, *In the Name of Jesus: Reflections on Christian Leadership* (New York: Crossroad, 1989), ix, x.

# Index

Foster, Richard, 53
fragmentation, role in teens' weakened respect for authority figures, 37–38
freedom, 12–13. *See also* real freedom
    expressions of, 48t
    giving, 157–58
    importance to teens, 47–51
    and Internet, 48
    from possessions, 105
    and relationships, 55, 56
    by religion and region, 48t
    from responsibility, 50
    from sin, 57
    and technology, 89
    through music, 69–70
free time, 62–63
French, John, 42
friendship. *See also* peer influence
    and honesty, 142–43
    importance by gender, 17t, 19t
    importance to teens of, 15–16, 15–16t, 20–21, 138t
    influence of, 17, 17t, 18–19, 19t, 51, 52, 83, 142, 158
    loss of, 15, 17t, 18, 19t, 112t
    as source of support, 15–16t
    stress of, 18, 52
    tribes and clans, 16–18, 20–21, 27–29, 31–32
friendship building, 26–27
friendship clans, 17–18, 29, 32, 65
friendship tribes, 17–18, 20–21, 23–24
*See also* peer influence
    and clothing, 17, 100
    cultural role of, 17
    held together by movies and television, 71–72
    and mocking, 117–18
    ostracism from, 15, 18
    unhealthy, 18–19, 52
    youth group as "a tribe apart," 27–29, 31–32, 157
future
    concern for, 83
    pressure about, 111, 112t, 118–19
    with God's guidance, 123–24
Galatians (New Testament book), 60
Gardner, Howard, 26

gender differences. *See* males vs. females
generalizations, about teenagers, 150, 151
generational differences, respecting, 91
generation gap, 20, 54
"generation on hold," 9
generosity, 19t, 59, 138t, 143, 143t
genocide, 141
Gerbner, George, 103
Gladwell, Malcolm, 23
Glenn, Stephen, 114–15, 151, 166n12
goal-setting, 124–25, 155–56
God. *See also* faith; Jesus; spirituality
    belief in, 113t, 125–26
    belief in a caring, 36, 36t
    compassion of, 55
    discussing, 144–45
    experienced by teens, 8, 36, 36t, 145–46
    and freedom, 57–59, 60–61
    influence of, 19t
    and love, 160, 161
    mystery of, 146–47
    reflected in human relationships, 24, 56
    regeneration through, 104
    as a relational deity, 20, 24, 31–32
    relationship with, 9, 27, 60, 62, 103, 104, 123–24
    as source of support, 16t
    teen perceptions of, 36, 36t
Goths, 100
government, weakened respect for leaders of, 34, 35t, 38
group loyalty, 45–46
group workers. See youth workers
group work, and power of community, 155–57

happiness, 113t, 113–14, 142
    through consumption, 100, 103, 113–14
hard work, importance of, 138t, 143t
Hersch, Patricia, 21, 112, 117
honesty, 16t, 138t, 143–44, 143t
    in behaviour, 138–39, 139t
    and friendship, 143–44